I'M NOT
REALLY
A WAITRESS

I'M NOT
REALLY
A WAITRESS

*How One Woman Revamped
the Beauty Industry One Color at a Time*

SUZI WEISS-FISCHMANN

SEAL PRESS

Seal Press
1700 Fourth Street
Berkeley, California 94710
@sealpress
Sealpress.com

Printed in the United States of America
Published by Seal Press, an imprint of Perseus Books, LLC, a subsidiary
of Hachette Book Group, Inc. The Seal Press name and logo is a trademark
of the Hachette Book Group.

The Hachette Speakers Bureau provides a wide range of authors for speaking events. To find out more, go to www.hachettespeakersbureau.com or
call (866) 376-6591.
The publisher is not responsible for websites (or their content) that are not
owned by the publisher.

Print book interior design by Linda Mark

Library of Congress Cataloging-in-Publication Data
Names: Weiss-Fischmann, Suzi, author.
Title: I'm not really a waitress : how one woman revamped the beauty
  industry one color at a time / Suzi Weiss-Fischmann.
Description: Berkeley, California. : Seal Press. [2019]
Identifiers: LCCN 2018032741 | ISBN 9781580058193 (hardcover) |
  ISBN 9781580058209 (e-book)
Subjects: LCSH: Weiss-Fischmann, Suzi. | OPI (Firm) | Cosmetics
  industry—United States. | Manicuring—Equipment and supplies. |
  Nail art (Manicuring) | Businesswomen—United States—Biography.
Classification: LCC HD9970.5.C674 O659 2019 | DDC 338.7/66855
  [B]—dc23
LC record available at https://lccn.loc.gov/2018032741
ISBNs: 978-1-58005-819-3 (hardcover), 978-1-58005-820-9 (ebook)

LSC-C

10 9 8 7 6 5 4 3 2 1

To my mom, my hero,
Magda Blau Weiss,
who endured the unendurable
and emerged loving, kind, and strong

CONTENTS

INTRODUCTION

A Great Opera-tunity

I USED TO BITE MY NAILS. CHRONICALLY, UNRESERVEDLY, obsessively.

I chewed on them any time I was nervous, and I was in the midst of gnawing a cuticle when the executive sitting across from me stopped his presentation. "Ms. Weiss," he said, "you know you have to stop that, right?" His look said it all: the co-owner and creative director of a global nail care brand couldn't very well go around with mangled nails.

It was 1991, just eighteen months after OPI had released a debut collection that was already revolutionizing the nail care industry. With bold, trendsetting colors like Malaga Wine and Coney Island Cotton Candy, OPI had made manicures the hot new fashion essential, and women everywhere were asking for OPI by name. Public relations guru Harris Shepard, who specialized in beauty and wellness brands, had taken notice and asked for a meeting. He was right about the nail-biting. Sheepishly, I nodded and sat on my hands.

I admit my mind wasn't entirely on Harris's presentation. Though I knew we'd created something special, no one had been prepared for such explosive growth. My co-founder George Schaeffer and I were working ten- and twelve-hour days, seven days a week. We hadn't given much thought to anything besides trying to keep up with customer demand, and I was anxious to get back to work. We sat through Harris's spiel, and then I asked for a moment to speak with George alone.

I've often wondered what must have gone through Harris's head as George and I ducked into the next room and launched into loud, rapid-fire Hungarian. He probably thought we were fighting to the death, but George and I always spoke this way. We'd worked together for years, first in New York City and then at OPI's headquarters in North Hollywood, in a shared office that was so small one of us had to sit behind our desk in order for the other to get through the door. And we were family. George was my brother-in-law, and we were both Hungarian immigrants who, like so many before us, had arrived in the United States with almost nothing, risking everything to pursue the American dream. He went on and on about all the possibilities of PR and what it could do for OPI before I was finally able to break in.

"George," I said, "this all sounds very nice—but what *is* pee-are?"

George, who has been silent for perhaps two minutes in the more than forty years I've known him, stared at me openmouthed for a full ten seconds. Then he burst out laughing. After wiping tears from his face he stuck his head back in the conference room. "One more minute, Mr. Shepard," he said. "We are *learning* something!" Then he collapsed into laughter again.

Apparently I felt sufficiently educated after that meeting, because we hired Mr. Shepard. No one could have known it at the time, but the three of us were about to be whisked away on a journey that would make many people's dreams come true and transform the beauty industry in ways none of us could have imagined. Our modest family business, which improbably enough had started as a dental supply company, would become the number-one professional salon brand in the world, famous for trendsetting colors; quirky, unforgettable names (every chapter and section title in this book is named after an OPI Nail Lacquer); and groundbreaking partnerships. We've teamed up with A-list celebrities, such as Justin Bieber, Carol Burnett, Mariah Carey, Selena Gomez, the Kardashian-Jenner clan, Cyndi Lauper, Jane Lynch, Nicki Minaj, Katy Perry, Gwen Stefani, Carrie Underwood, Kerry Washington, and Serena Williams, and global lifestyle brands ranging from Coca-Cola and Hello Kitty! to Sony's *Skyfall* 007 Bond franchise, from

Disney to Ford Motor Company to Dell, to create exclusive nail lacquer collections.

The OPI family would grow from George and me and our immediate families, who showed up to help fill, label, and package bottles by hand, to more than seven hundred employees housed on a seven-acre campus. Together we'd create a beauty icon that even after more than thirty-seven years in the notoriously fickle beauty industry is a bestseller in more than one hundred countries.

The OPI journey continues to be a grand, improbable adventure. I have no doubt it has fashioned me into the person I was meant to be. Harris Shepard, that inscrutable purveyor of "pee-are," has now been my best friend for more than twenty-five years, and perhaps he puts it best when he says that OPI led me to become my true self. From Zsuzsi Weiss, the shy, reserved schoolgirl who fled fear and oppression and arrived in this country with no English and little means, to Suzi the First Lady of Nails, the entrepreneur who put her passions for color and beauty to work to give women everywhere an unlimited means of self-expression, to Suzi Weiss-Fischmann, the wife and mother who—with a great deal of help—still did carpool and made it to family dinners and school plays while running a multimillion-dollar business.

As you will see, if I can do this, anyone can. And yes, I even learned to stop biting my nails.

one

SUZI WITHOUT A PADDLE

W<small>E FLED UNDER COVER OF NIGHT.</small>
It was 1966 and I was ten years old, and for years the Hungarian Secret Police had been pressuring my father to become an informant. This was just part of life under the Communist system. Everyone was encouraged to spy on each other, and those who could deliver information were rewarded with favors such as better housing or shorter waits for goods like cars, televisions, or meat. As it could take five years or more to get a car, most people were highly motivated to provide information.

The Secret Police would consider anything, but they were especially interested in knowing if people were coming and going from your house, or if you'd received any packages, or if you appeared to have more than your neighbor—more food, more livestock, better clothing. Under the Communist system no one was to have any more than anyone else. Indeed, two years before, the Communist Party had decided that our two-bedroom, one-bathroom house was too much for a four-person family, so they moved a family of three in with us. What I remember more than the cramped quarters was how my family spoke in whispers after that, afraid our new housemates were spies. My parents had already endured the horrors of the Holocaust—my mother had survived Auschwitz, and my father had been captured by the Germans on the Russian front and put in a forced labor camp, where his brother had been killed—so they were well acquainted with spying and betrayal. And, as *kulaks*—landowners—we were already under constant surveillance, which helped explain why my father had long been a special target of the Secret Police.

There was also the matter of food. Because my father was a butcher we had access to meat. We owned a few cows and chickens, and we grew grapes. My mother also had a cousin in New York City who occasionally sent us packages containing hand-me-down clothes, American toilet paper—a true luxury compared to the stiff, scratchy Communist-issue stuff—and aluminum foil, which we gathered around and gazed upon, amazed. In every package the cousin included the American candy M&Ms, which my mother would collect in a jar and then ration, giving my older sister Miriam and me a few precious pieces a day.

The Secret Police's tactics were always the same: they arrived without warning in the middle of the night. Each time, they'd try to persuade my father to become an informant for the Communist Party, and each time he would resist. The consequence was always jail. Because he could pay a bribe to get out, he was usually detained only for a night.

Then one morning everything changed. Miriam and I woke to find our mother missing. As we were to learn, the Secret Police had come in the night and taken her. They'd directed her to bring some clothes and a bucket. The clothes meant she'd be gone for days. The bucket was for relieving herself.

Leaving us in the care of a housekeeper, my father hurried to the police station to try and bring my mother home. It was the most frightened I'd ever seen him. As odd as it sounds now, we'd become somewhat accustomed to his arrests—and he always returned. But my mother . . . this was unheard of. My father knew at once that her arrest was a message intended for him. *Cooperate, or your family pays the price.*

For three days he begged the police to release her, offering more and more money each time, and finally they accepted. She came home on the fourth day.

That was when my father began making plans for our escape.

Chasing Rainbows

In Judaism there is a concept known as *tzedakah*. It can be translated as "charity," but the true meaning goes much deeper. It is a sacred act of giving back, of enacting justice in the world. *Tzedakah* is both an obligation and a privilege. When we have the opportunity, we are to help others—just as we will be helped from time to time. Throughout life we will be both the recipient and the giver of acts of generosity.

I'll never know the many acts of *tzedakah* that enabled my parents first to escape the camps and, later, imprisonment (and worse) by the Hungarian Secret Police. What I do know is that somehow, despite all they endured, they were the very embodiment of *tzedakah*: warm, loving, generous people. Even in the environment of fear and intimidation in Hungary, I was raised in a home full of warmth, by parents whose love was unfailing.

When my father met with an official in order to obtain passports for our entire family, he had one question: "HOW MUCH?"

I am sure acts of *tzedakah* were at work during my family's escape from Hungary as well. All I knew at the time, however, was our cover story: we told everyone we were moving to Budapest so Miriam, age sixteen, could enroll in a good high school. We sold our house to a doctor, who, because he held a high rank in the party, promptly evicted the family who'd been living with us and had the house all to himself.

Despite the plausible cover story, we packed and left in the middle of the night, fearful of being detained. We drove fifty miles west from our home in Gyöngyös to the capital, Budapest, and moved into a one-room apartment. My father arranged to meet with a Ministry official, a man he'd known from his childhood village, so we could obtain four passports. To prevent escape, the Communist Party never allowed entire families to travel together—at least one person had to remain behind. Getting passports for all four of us was highly irregular, so when my father met with the official he had only one question: "How much?" He paid an exorbitant sum, and then there was nothing to do but wait for the passports to come through.

That was a time of terrible anxiety and isolation. Because my parents didn't want anyone asking us questions, they didn't enroll Miriam and me in school, and we only left the apartment when absolutely necessary. We could go out a little at night, and if anyone happened to ask us about ourselves, Miriam and I pretended we'd been in school all day like other children. The one exception to our isolation was that in another extraordinary act of generosity, a kind rabbi visited our apartment in secret. We'd close all the blinds when he arrived, and he taught us to pray and read in Hebrew.

After what seemed an eternity the passports arrived, and once again we made a nighttime escape. We took only what we could fit in a few suitcases. My father's best friend, a man who'd been in the forced labor camp with him and who had settled in Budapest, came to get us. He and his wife drove us to the airport, and I can clearly remember these two brave men embracing as they said goodbye, and my father's friend crying as he left us. They knew they would never see each other again.

There is no way to describe the terror we felt as we went through passport control. The officials had us file through one by one, my mother first, then Miriam, then me. After each person was scrutinized and her passport stamped, we were directed to another room, which left us unable to see the rest of the family. Miriam and my mother and I began to despair when many long minutes passed with no sign of my father. We were shaking when he was finally permitted through, convinced he'd been detained. But we all had to maintain an outward demeanor of calm, as if we were a family just going off on holiday. No one relaxed until we were out of Hungarian air space.

We landed in Athens, Greece, where an Israeli relief organization was waiting to meet us. Again I marveled at the preparations my parents had been up to—my mother's cousins had connections with the relief organization, and she'd somehow arranged for them to help us. They took us to a hotel, where we stayed until a ship bound for Israel arrived. After a three-day journey, in which I was violently seasick the entire time, we landed at Haifa, where more of my mother's cousins were waiting.

I will never forget my first glimpse of Israel. We arrived just as the sun was rising over Haifa. The golden dome of the Shrine of the Báb was afire with sunlight, surrounded by gleaming white buildings, and beyond, the evergreen-covered Mount Carmel mountain range loomed. It was so beautiful it brought tears to my eyes.

We lived with the cousins in Holon until we found our own apartment there. My father found work as a butcher, and shortly thereafter I took on my very first job—of sorts. My mother got a job cleaning a bank at night. More to be near her than anything else, I would go with her and help mop the floors. That job didn't last, however, as she was constantly setting off the panic button by accident. The bank manager and the police grew tired of coming out every night, and we were unceremoniously let go. Eventually my mother found work watching children in a private home, which mercifully had no panic button.

Life in Israel could not have been more different from life in Communist Hungary. Whereas Hungary was all about uniformity and intimidation, moving to Israel was a little like Dorothy's transition from Kansas to Oz—everything seemed to be in full, vibrant color. The air was fresh and clean, we could play outside, there was no fear of Secret Police or spying neighbors, we

> *Moving from Communist Hungary to Israel was like Dorothy's move from Kansas to Oz—suddenly THE WORLD WAS IN FULL, VIBRANT COLOR.*

could practice our faith openly, and we were all agog at the vast array of choices available. Our first trip to a market was overwhelming. There wasn't one brand of coffee but three. Not one type of bread but three or four, all fresh and delicious. Whereas before an orange had been a rare treat, the markets in Israel were overflowing with mounds of fresh fruits and vegetables. There was no longer any need for rationing or waiting in interminable lines, no need for working hard to preserve and store enough food to get through the winters. In Israel all we had to do was pop down to the market. It all seemed like a miracle.

Our transition wasn't without its difficulties, however. We were strangers in a strange land who knew no Hebrew beyond what we'd learned from prayers. For me, fifth grade got off to a rough start. I'd hoped to blend into the background, but when I showed up to school in a Communist schoolgirl's little pleated skirt and starched blouse I couldn't have looked any more out of place. Then, when my teacher summoned me to the front of the room to introduce me to the class, I spontaneously got a terrible nosebleed! I wasn't used to the dry air, and there I stood, mortified, blood dripping onto my starched white blouse. I tried my best to clean it but I had to wear the stained shirt all day. As if all that wasn't bad enough, on my way home that afternoon boys threw eggs at me, which hit my head and cracked, leaving me terrified, crying, and covered in egg yolk. Having been raised by such positive parents I'm normally quite an optimistic person, but to this day I still remember the shock and the humiliation of that incident. Word got around about it, though, and a kindhearted teacher admonished the boys. No one ever bothered me again.

Nomad's Dream

Soon enough, I discovered certain benefits to the highly disciplined Communist education system I'd been brought up in, where everyone was expected to live and perform at the highest standard—if not perfection. For one, I was completely comfortable with memorization and with studying for many hours, which enabled me to pick up Hebrew relatively quickly. I don't think I was ever the most brilliant student in the classroom, but I did possess the ability to work hard and stick with something until I got it. This kind of discipline helped me many times in life.

Another huge benefit, ironically enough, was the assumption that girls and women were capable of anything. It was hardly Communism's intent to foster a bunch of feminists, but here's the blunt truth: in Hungary in that day and age under Communist rule, many of the men turned to alcohol, which was one of the few things in plentiful supply. With so many men spending their days drinking, the women were left to do everything. So I grew up seeing women as the doctors and scientists and engineers and lawyers and architects—all while managing households as well. I grew up knowing that girls and women were capable of accomplishing anything they set out to do. Later in life this set of assumptions would figure directly into my career path, but right then as a student in Israel, I had the supreme advantage of confidence: it never once occurred to me that I couldn't master

> *It was hardly Communism's intent to foster a bunch of feminists, but I grew up seeing women as the doctors and scientists and engineers and lawyers and architects.*
> *I never once doubted that GIRLS AND WOMEN WERE CAPABLE OF ANYTHING.*

this new language and this new culture if I just worked hard enough.

Once I was fluent in the language, I was able to do well in school and make friends. The world opened up to me, and I was the happiest I'd ever been. I loved everything about Israel, which to my young mind seemed a land of total freedom. You could leave your house any time you wanted. You could practice your religion in peace. You could play outside for many hours, with no fear. You could say anything you wanted, to anyone you wanted, with no fear of hidden microphones or lurking spies. It was unbelievable to me that we didn't have to whisper at home or go around town with our eyes downcast, hurrying to get back indoors. Even when the Six-Day War broke out and emergency sirens wailed and residents were forced to take cover in bunkers, I absolutely loved Israel.

America called to so many with its siren song of freedom, safety, and opportunity for those who worked hard. My father was one of them, and WE JOINED A GREAT THRONG WHO MOVED TO AMERICA FOR A BETTER LIFE.

For my parents, however, this was a time of great uncertainty. Their intention was to remain in Israel just long enough to get our green cards and move to America—perhaps six months, tops. Everyone knew that only in America was it possible to start with nothing and end with great success, if only you worked hard. This was the irresistible siren song that called to so many people all over the world, and my father was one of them. He wanted freedom and safety for his family, the opportunity to make a new life for us, and the chance for his daughters to create the same for their future families.

But as defectors from a Communist country, getting green cards proved tougher than we'd anticipated. At that time America was, to say the least, deeply wary of Communists, and after such a huge influx of Hungarians following the revolution in 1956, the government had instituted a quota system. The process was first come, first served, so all we could do was get in line and wait for our numbers to come up. My parents could not plan on anything because our number could come up literally at any time.

After six months, that's just what happened—but only for one of us. Miriam would be permitted to travel to the States to attend high school. We didn't want to be separated but no one turned down an opportunity to go to America, and we thought we'd join her shortly after she left anyway. She moved in with some of my mother's cousins in New York City, so we knew she was safe in the meantime. But then the weeks and months kept accumulating, and my parents were summoned multiple times for interviews at the American embassy. Miriam would call from time to time, wondering where we were and what was taking so long, but we had no answers to give.

Because learning Hebrew had proved much harder for my parents, I accompanied them to the embassy so I could translate. The Americans' questions were surprisingly detailed. They would ask about specific dates and times when party meetings were held, and they wanted

to know if my father had attended. Or, they would begin by assuming he'd attended, and they'd want to know
what went on at the meeting. His answers were always
the same—no, he hadn't attended any meetings, and he
kept insisting that this was the very reason we were in
Israel, because he hadn't wanted any part of the Communist Party! After a while I didn't even bother translating
and just answered the questions myself. That was when
the embassy officials relieved me of my translation duties.

In the end it took two and a half years for our interloc-
utors to be satisfied that my parents weren't Communist
spies. But finally we were permitted to leave. Yet again we
packed our belongings and left, bracing ourselves to learn
another new culture. This time it would be for good.

Big Apple Red

When we were finally reunited with Miriam we could
hardly believe our eyes. She was no longer a gangly ado-
lescent but a young lady of nineteen. She had really flour-
ished in New York City and loved it there. She'd worked
as a camp counselor each summer in the Catskills, she
was dating, she had lots of American friends, and she was
fluent in English . . . she was an American!

The four of us settled in the neighborhood of Forest
Hills in Queens. Our apartment was nice but small, with
one bedroom, one bathroom, and a kitchen. Miriam and
I slept on a sofa bed in the living room. We lived together
in that apartment for the next three and a half years, until
Miriam moved out in 1972 to get married. I would remain

there with my parents for another twelve years, when I moved out in pursuit of a career.

But in 1969, my parents and I faced a difficult adjustment. Again there was a new language to learn, and as I was now almost fourteen, it wasn't as easy this time. Every day after school I stayed late to attend English classes. Again I faced the same scenario of being teased because I was different, except this time it wasn't an isolated experience on the first day of school but the daily nuisance of boys who blew spitballs in my hair. But once again my strong sense of discipline and excellent study habits came to the rescue. I put

In Hungary there were no choices when it came to style—we all dressed alike. But IN NEW YORK, ANYTHING WAS POSSIBLE, and I saw that one's personality could instantly be broadcast through style.

them to good use to learn English as fast as I could so I could get out of those dreaded after-school classes with those dreadful boys.

I was also supremely determined to learn English so I could fit in and be like the other kids. It was in New York City that I took my very first steps toward cultivating my own sense of style. Looking back, I think I always had an affinity for beauty, whether it was a gorgeous sunset or a work of art or a lovely fabric. But it wasn't until we moved to America that I gained both the maturity and the opportunity to pay attention to things like fashion, style, color, and self-expression. In Hungary there simply were no choices when it came to style—we all dressed alike and the government suppressed freedom of expression in any form. In Israel there was more choice, but I was still young, and playing outside and relishing freedom took precedence over everything else.

But in New York, everywhere I looked there were millions of people with millions of individual styles. I saw that one's personality could instantly be broadcast through one's fashion choices, and I saw that first impressions were of great importance. In no more than a moment, you could discern a great deal about people by what they wore. Put another way, people size you up—they judge you—at a glance. I caught on quickly that the way I was dressing wasn't going to get me anywhere.

What did my look say? Still in my pressed skirts and starched blouses, buttoned all the way up to my chin, I came across as an awkward little girl. In fact, that is what a stranger once called me when Miriam was showing me around Manhattan. After she ducked into a store and I stood on the sidewalk nearly stupefied at all the noise and activity, I bolstered my courage to practice my English, and I asked a passerby where the Empire State Building was. He stared at me incredulously. "Little girl," he said, "look up!" I followed his pointing finger to see the Empire State Building looming right over us.

So, yes, I looked and acted like what I was: an overwhelmed, awkward little girl. Don't forget that this was 1969, and hippie culture, with its flowing caftans and psychedelic prints and bell bottoms, was one of the dominant style influences. One glance at me telegraphed that I was a fish out of water.

An Israeli-born friend helped me adjust. Anat's family had moved to the United States when she was a child, so she had grown up in the States and thoroughly knew the lay of the land. We bonded quickly, and I began to explore my own sense of style by first emulating hers. She wore jeans—all new to me—and encouraged me to unfasten a button or two on my blouse. She and I routinely stopped in front of Bloomingdale's window displays, where I feasted upon a veritable riot of color, with styles that just blew my mind. There's no telling how many times I stood there gazing longingly at the dresses on the mannequins, imagining a time when I could wear such things.

And in fact, when I was fifteen and got my first job— at a Dairy Queen—right away I started to become a little fashionista. For the first time I had my own money, and I saved my paychecks to buy clothes—*new* clothes! Not worn-out hand-me-downs, which more often than not I simply didn't like, but store-bought, brand-new clothes of my own choosing. This was a rarity, as all of my clothes were hand-me-downs from my sister and cousins. (The exception was shoes, as my feet were bigger than Miriam's and I couldn't squeeze into her old shoes.) But of course, my Dairy Queen earnings weren't all that much, so I would wait and wait and wait for the outfits in the department store windows to go on sale . . . and by the time I could afford them, most of the time my size was no longer in stock.

Every now and again, however, I got lucky. And because I was patient, I was able to wait for just the right thing. To me it was better to wait for that one very special thing than to spend right now on any old thing I could afford. That habit stuck with me for life: to this day I'd still rather have one very good quality, timeless piece than ten trendy things that happen to hit the stores.

That said, it's a toss-up whether the best perk of the Dairy Queen job was the paycheck or the free ice cream. Ice cream has always been my favorite food above all others, and even in Hungary, my mother would try to get ice cream for me. At Dairy Queen I found myself enjoying the unbelievable luxury of daily ice cream. I'm now in my sixties, and I've dined in the world's finest restaurants and tasted the creations of the world's best pastry chefs. But still, give me a bowl of vanilla chocolate chip any day. Ice cream is the one area of my life in which I have absolutely no discipline whatsoever. I cannot have it in my house, as I will eat the entire carton in one sitting.

If Hungary was about fear, Israel was about freedom, and AMERICA WAS ABOUT LIMITLESS POSSIBILITY. You could start over in America and be anything and anyone you wanted to be.

Suffice it to say, life was very good in the United States. We were safe, we were together, and my parents could finally put down roots and start building a life. My father found work as a butcher and my mother was a homemaker. Meanwhile with the help of after-school ESL classes I learned English, I made friends, I earned a little money, and I began to glimpse the wide range of possibilities available in the world. If Hungary was about fear, Israel was about freedom, and America was about limitless possibility. This really was the land of opportunity—you could start over in America and be anything you wanted to be. This was why my parents had risked everything to get us here. After all we'd been through, we were keenly aware of how fortunate we were.

Life proceeded apace, in a refreshingly normal way. Miriam and I studied hard and did well in school. She graduated from college with a degree in accounting, and after high school I enrolled at Hunter College in New York City. I majored in biology and intended to work in a lab after graduation, dreaming of inventing a cure for some terrible disease.

But fate was soon to intervene, and it arrived in the form of a blind date between my sister and another Hungarian immigrant, a man who'd also escaped with his family and ended up in New York City, heeding the clarion call of the American dream.

two

THIS COLOR'S MAKING WAVES

THE TREMENDOUS KNOCK AT OUR APARTMENT DOOR RAT-tled the windowpanes. My father opened the door to find a twenty-five-year-old guy with a wide smile and a huge Afro. This was George Schaeffer, my sister Miriam's blind date.

The date had been arranged in true Old World style by an old lady in our neighborhood, a mutual acquaintance of my mother and George's mother, who thought it was high time this nice young man settle down and marry. Like us George was a Hungarian immigrant. He had arrived in the United States in 1956 after his family fled the Hungarian Revolution. Nine-year-old George and his parents packed what they could and walked more than thirty miles into Austria, where an American relief organization helped arrange their passage to the States. They crossed the ocean on a B-52 bomber and landed at JFK.

George absolutely filled the room, and not just because it was a small apartment and he was a big guy. Even then George had abundant charisma, a quick mind, and a loud laugh. With his natural charm and kindness, it was no wonder he was already a successful salesman. George's family owned a garment business called Rosemary Underwear Manufacturing Company. It had begun like so many immigrant endeavors: with one person who worked very hard. Rosemary's roots lay with George's mother. She started by sewing half-slips by hand at home, eventually got a sewing machine and a little shop, and by the time we met George in 1972, the business had grown to a factory of some two hundred employees that made undergarments, women's blouses, and quilted robes. It was a true family business, with George as the head of sales, his father as CPA, and his mother as head of operations.

My parents absolutely loved George. We all did. Besides his warmth and generosity, he was 100 percent real— there were no pretensions about him. But one of the best things about George, especially as far as my parents were concerned, was our common cultural and linguistic heritage. It's difficult to convey how important this is to an immigrant. My parents' English was never great (my dad was fifty-four when he arrived in the States), and here was a man with whom they could easily converse and connect. To them, George was a taste of home.

In short, we all just *got* each other, and George's courtship with Miriam was brief but intense. Within three months they were married, and it wasn't just Miriam's life that changed after the wedding. For the first time in my life, I had a bed all to myself, which at the time was an unimaginable luxury. And I said goodbye to my beloved summer job at Dairy Queen and began working at Rosemary Manufacturing. You could say this was my first job in the fashion industry, though it was certainly far from glamorous! Every day after school I took the subway to 657 Broadway and Bleecker Street, where I'd stand for hours preparing orders for shipping. My job was to group hanging shirts together by the dozen and then insert a ticket with a tagging gun. Over and over and over, I'd gather eleven shirts on wire hangers, finish it off with the twelfth, reach over to hook them together, punch in a ticket, and move on to the next. It was repetitive, monotonous work, and I'd do that for hours and then go home and do homework.

Miriam, meanwhile, with her degree in accounting, worked in the payroll department with George's father. And every Friday, she and I gathered the factory overruns of junior tops and sold them to the factory workers for a deep discount. Once when she went on vacation, I took over her payroll duties. I didn't have a clue what I was doing, and that Friday I found myself staring down a long line of angry workers whose paychecks I'd bungled.

George's father was so mad at me. That was the first and last time I ever worked in payroll.

I kept my job at Rosemary for the remainder of high school and then all the way through my four years at Hunter College. At Hunter I majored in biology, and for a time I pictured myself going to work in a research lab, peering through a microscope and maybe contributing to cancer research. But a seed had been planted at Rosemary Manufacturing that ended up changing the trajectory of my life. Though I wouldn't fully appreciate the value of this for a long time—especially while I was hanging shirts by the dozen and sweeping the factory floor—what I'd been given was a front-row seat to witness how to launch and run a successful entrepreneurial venture. I couldn't have received a better introduction to business. The Schaeffers had arrived in this country with little money, no contacts, and no English. But they had intelligence, a strong work ethic, and tenacity. I saw what hard work could accomplish, and after adapting to two different cultures and languages before I was out of adolescence, I knew I had it in me to work that hard, too. If they could do this, so could I.

Working at Rosemary and learning from the Schaeffers also gave me a glimpse of what it was like to control one's own destiny. From a very early age I knew I wanted to make money because I'd witnessed how it could influence events and make things happen, even to the point of saving a life. It was money that had opened the jail cell doors for my parents, after all, and money that had arranged for our safe passage out of a dangerous place. So, even when I was quite young, I understood money to be a means to freedom and autonomy. It gave you power and, possibilities that weren't available otherwise.

A successful business also meant being able to provide a better life for your family and your employees and, in turn, their families. Rosemary, for example, was built by people who never forgot their humble beginnings and tried to extend that same chance to others. I remember while I was still a teenager seeing George give money to homeless people. It was a routine practice

NEVER MISS AN OPPORTUNITY TO HELP SOMEONE if you're in a position to do so. You never know the long-term impact it will have.

for him, and he happened to strike up a passing acquaintanceship with a homeless man he saw on a daily basis. One day George asked him what he'd done formerly, and he replied that he repaired machines—he could fix any machine, in fact. George nodded once and told him to be at 657 Broadway the next morning at 7 a.m. The man showed up, and repaired a broken sewing machine, and George hired him on the spot. From then on George picked him up from the Bowery every day on his way to work, and this gentleman worked at Rosemary for years, repairing sewing machines, button markers, or any other small machinery that broke down.

That's what I mean about the value of having money and being in a position to help. If you had resources, you could directly and profoundly improve people's lives. And if it's just one person, that is enough! You've done something right, and you have made a true difference. It's a lesson I never forgot, and it would figure directly into how we later operated OPI.

But of course, that would be years down the road. What was clear to me at the time was that this is where I first got the idea that I wanted to go into business for myself. It was at Rosemary that my entrepreneurial spirit was sparked. So, after college, instead of a white coat and a research lab, I donned factory clothes and went to work at Rosemary full-time. As the years went on my duties expanded and I learned multiple aspects of how to run a business. I gained a deep understanding of the factory workers' experience because I was one of them, and I learned administrative duties, infrastructure, sales, distribution, you name it. Everything except payroll!

George and I discovered that we worked very well together. We were so similar in so many ways that people often mistook us for brother and sister—as they would for many years. We were both deeply driven and disciplined and willing to tackle anything, no matter how steep the learning curve. And somehow our personalities—his extroverted and gregarious, mine more introverted and reserved—complemented each other and meshed well. We couldn't have known it at the time, of course, but these years in my teens and early twenties were forging one of the most unlikely powerhouse business partnerships ever, a brother-in-law and sister-in-law Hungarian entrepreneurial team.

Stars in My Eyes

As the 1980s approached, things began to change at Rosemary and for many other businesses in the garment industry. It was becoming increasingly difficult to do business in New York City, as there was a lot of competition from exports from the Far East that could be produced far more inexpensively. With rising costs, it was becoming more of a struggle to pay rent, make payroll, and manufacture, and George saw the writing on the wall. It was clear that producing low-end blouses and undergarments wasn't going to be sustainable for the long term. So, in mid-1980 when he got a call from his uncle in California who wanted to sell his business and retire, George flew out to check it out.

Located in a dime-a-dozen strip mall, Ondontorium Products, Incorporated, was a small outfit that manufactured and sold dental products and supplies. George didn't know a thing about the dental industry, but he did know that Rosemary's future was tenuous, and he certainly knew how to sell anything. Plus, who can beat the Southern California weather? So, after just a little consideration he bought the company, and he and Miriam and their two-year-old son Robbie moved to Los Angeles.

By this time I was twenty-five years old and had worked with George for a decade. It was only natural that I would consider joining him at this new venture. The switch from the fashion industry to the dental industry was admittedly bizarre, but like George I had a can-do spirit, and I knew if I applied myself and worked hard

I could learn anything. So I never even thought twice about going to work for this Ondontorium Products business, whatever it turned out to be. I was still living with my parents then. We decided that I'd go check it out, and if I liked the work I would join George and Miriam in California, and my parents would follow some time later.

That was my first trip to the west coast of America, and I couldn't believe my eyes as I took in Southern California. With its palm trees and bright sunshine and warm climate, there was something reminiscent of my beloved time in Israel. And the colors! Just as in Haifa, I was drawn to the colors of Southern California like a bee to honey—the green palms, the sparkling Pacific that could take on the color of the sky, the brilliant orange of California poppy. I was absolutely intoxicated by the warm weather, the friendly people, and the abundance of color, and I knew immediately I wanted to move. When I got back to New York I described California to my parents in enraptured terms, and we began making plans for my move. Meanwhile George was arranging for the closure of Rosemary. I made a couple more visits to California to get the lay of the land, and at the end of 1981 I packed a single suitcase, got on a plane, and moved to L.A. My father, apparently assuming I was moving to California to be some sort of junior-level assistant, left me with these parting words of advice: "Don't fuck up the coffee when they ask you."

And then on January 1, 1982, at the age of twenty-six, I went to work for Ondontorium Products, Incorporated. I didn't have the slightest clue what was about to hit me. No one did.

Back in the Saddle

For the first eight or nine months in California I lived with George and Miriam and little Robbie, as I couldn't afford my own place. Eventually I got an apartment on Fulton Avenue in Sherman Oaks. It was an unfurnished one-bedroom, and though I still didn't have much money, I was incredibly excited to decorate my own place according to my own taste for the very first time. I wanted simple, modern, and chic, but it had to be affordable. There was one solution: IKEA.

When the furniture arrived a couple of Ondontorium Products employees came over to help me, as I was great at selecting stylish items but useless at reading instructions and assembling anything. I allowed myself one indulgence that was well within my skill set: I always had fresh flowers in the apartment. It's a habit I never gave up.

At work, I did a little bit of everything. (That did not, however, include payroll, making coffee, or assembling furniture.) I did administrative tasks, worked in sales, helped customers, took orders, and ordered supplies. I was also a "picker" at the warehouse. If a dental technician arrived, I'd help him try and match dentures, and then I'd go to the warehouse and fetch the product from inventory. I remember rooting through drawers and drawers of false teeth.

But meanwhile, something far more interesting than dentures was happening at Ondontorium Products, Inc. George had already noticed that it wasn't just dental technicians who were showing up to buy dental supplies—we also got a steady stream of decidedly more glamorous clientele. With just a few questions, he learned they were Hollywood nail technicians and salon owners, and they were buying dental acrylics in order to make their own artificial nail extensions. Remember this was the '80s, and long, talon-like nails were all the rage among Hollywood celebrities. It turned out that dentures and artificial nail extensions shared a very similar chemistry.

So, within my first few months on the job, George was describing a whole new area of potential to explore. If we could formulate and manufacture a product that was superior to the nail techs' DIY efforts, there would be a huge opportunity in the nail business. I admit that at first I had no idea what he was talking about. Fake teeth and fake nails? What were we doing?!

But again I knew I could do any task life threw at me as long as I worked hard, and I trusted George's instincts. I was in.

We began by researching the products that were already available. We learned that one major flaw of many of the DIY nail acrylics was that if the nail extension happened to snag on something it could rip off, which could result in severe and even permanent damage to the underlying nail bed. So one of our first priorities was making a *safer* product—something that would not only last but wouldn't damage the natural nail and would maybe even protect it.

And of course, we wanted to make a product that was in every way of better quality than anything else on the market. We wanted to make the best professional product out there and address the professional nail technicians' needs better than anyone else did. The materials used to make artificial nails at the time consisted of a liquid primer, a polymer powder, and a liquid monomer. After this mixture was applied and exposed to oxygen it began to harden, so the technician had limited time to file the nail to the desired shape and length. We wanted a product that would flow perfectly, require less filing, and dry completely in a shorter period of time. In short, we wanted to create a product that would be everything the professional nail technician could ever hope for.

Put another way, we set out to become *the* go-to brand for nail care professionals. This was part of our original vision, and we never strayed from it.

This is a point worth lingering over, especially for anyone considering going into business for themselves or taking on a risky endeavor. Remember that we knew absolutely nothing about the science of creating artificial nails. What we did know was that we'd identified an opportunity in the market that was ripe for the taking. There was already a demand for a better product, as evidenced by the nail techs who were buying our dental

Before we even knew how to make nail polish, WE SET OUT TO BE THE NAIL CARE BRAND FOR PROFESSIONALS. This goal was part of our original vision, and we never once forgot it.

supplies to create their own nails. So, once we identified that opportunity and committed to it, we simultaneously committed to becoming no less than the best, no matter what it took to get there. We wanted to elevate the entire industry.

A very wise person once said, "A business without a vision isn't a business. It's a pastime." I couldn't agree more. Our vision was a huge motivating factor, and it would sustain us through however long it took to formulate a product that would be the best of the best, in an area that we didn't know well and would have to learn as we went.

To take over the tasks that were completely out of our area of expertise—the science—we hired a young polymer chemist who specialized in creating special effects for the movie industry. And then came two long years of testing and retesting and tweaking and retweaking our formula. (In the meantime, my parents moved to California, and I taught myself how to make acrylic nails by using my mother as my guinea pig.)

This was a time of great uncertainty for us, as we weren't making any money and there was zero guarantee we'd succeed. We were also still running the dental business at the same time. One of the dental firm's employees, a very smart man named Bryan Stein who did material information systems, no doubt wondered what on earth these crazy new owners were up to and if he should get out while the getting was good. Two years is obviously a long time to go without being profitable. Here is where a strong vision you believe in deeply is so crucial. George and I were united in a common goal, we had the same drive for perfection, and we were convinced we could do it. So, like the Energizer Bunny, we just . . . kept . . . going.

As for Bryan, apparently he was convinced as well. He stuck around for the long term, as you will see.

Finally we were convinced we had it. The result was a three-bottle system consisting of a polymer powder, a liquid monomer, and a primer that had to be applied in the correct order, and at the right intervals, which meant we needed to educate the salon owners and nail technicians about how to use this brand-new product. Our plan was to hand-deliver our system to salon owners and nail professionals, show them how to use it, and then go back in a few weeks to see how they liked it.

Or more correctly, *I* would be doing that. Most of the salon owners at that time were women, and George thought I'd have a better chance of connecting with them, woman to woman. I agreed, but I wondered aloud how I'd carry around multiple sets of three bottles. George shrugged and said, "Put a rubber band around it."

And that is how the now-legendary Rubber Band Special—the prototype of the OPI Traditional Acrylic System—was born.

With ordinary rubber bands we scrounged from our desks, we bound the three-bottle sets together with an instruction sheet. It wasn't pretty but it was efficient and effective. I walked up and down Ventura Boulevard in L.A. hand-delivering Rubber Band Specials to salon owners. I showed them how to use it, and I told everyone we were a new company that was manufacturing a new acrylic nail product, making sure to drop the name "OPI." If the salon owners liked our product, they'd know to ask for OPI by name.

The change in name—from the clunky "Ondon-torium Products, Incorporated" to the more sleek and memorable "OPI"—had come about as something of a joke. George and I had kicked around a few possibilities for our new brand, but nothing stuck. Then at the end of a particularly long and discouraging day, when we were facing the very real possibility that our new company could be short-lived, we decided simply to shorten its name to OPI. And that's the ultra-sexy story of how this now-iconic brand name was born.

For two weeks we waited nervously (I mangled my nails) waiting for the salon owners to try the product. And then the response blew us away. Every single nail professional who tried the Rubber Band Special said it was the best acrylic system they'd ever used. One hundred percent. Everyone wanted more, and they all asked where they could buy it. This was it. We'd done it.

So, back at "headquarters," we ramped up production of the Rubber Band Special, renamed it the OPI Traditional Acrylic System, and got it in the hands of as many salon owners as possible. The next time I checked in with them, they told me they couldn't keep it in stock.

Raisin' the Bar

Confident we were really onto something, it was time to start winding down the dental supply side of the business and transitioning to the beauty industry. But we also needed to capitalize on all the momentum we had going and ex-pand—I couldn't very well continue hand-delivering our product to salons. So George and I educated ourselves about how the professional beauty industry worked, and we realized that to expand in the way we wanted to—which for us meant establishing a long-term business rather than pursuing short-term profits or quick expansion— we needed to work with salespeople, sales representative firms, and distributors. In practical terms, this

> *In person or online, building relationships is absolutely key to a successful business. YOUR WORD IS YOUR GOLD and your brand is your trust.*

meant we wouldn't sell directly to salons anymore; instead we'd establish ourselves with distributors and they would be the link between us and the salons.

Though "distributors" may sound impersonal, these were really old family businesses that had begun as mom-and-pop stores and were passed on to the next generation. The beauty distributors all knew each other, and they had a shared history that went back decades. We realized that part of becoming successful in this arena would require becoming acquainted with all of these people and establishing relationships—which just happened to be how George and I liked to do business.

This is something I emphasize to any young person going into business today. Building relationships is absolutely key! Even though so much of connecting and communicating is done online now, there are still people behind every keyboard and smartphone, and each one represents an opportunity for you to distinguish yourself from your competitors and make your product known.

Much of OPI's success was built upon our attention to cultivating good relationships with anyone who would be touched by the business. From suppliers to the sales force to the maintenance crew, and later in our journey, from fashion editors to public relations pros to celebrity trend-setters—and above all, to the *consumer*—our business was built on relationships.

Here is a plain and simple fact: people respond to people. People invest in people. Even in your personal life, you respond better to someone when you are in relationship with them. Think about the times you need advice or a second opinion. Whose words are more valuable—those of a trusted friend, or a stranger? In business it's the same thing, and this is why taking the time to interact with anyone involved with the business is so important. Loyalty goes a long way, especially when you're beginning your business. Your word is your gold and your brand is your trust.

So our next step was to hire a sales repping firm, which would help us get to know the distributors, who would then help us build relationships with salon owners. The first firm represented us in the thirteen western states—California, Idaho, Utah, Colorado, Oregon, Washington, Arizona, Alaska, Nevada, New Mexico, Montana, Hawaii, and Wyoming. They thought we were onto something amazing, but again, George and I prepared ourselves not to make any money for the first two years. We said fine, we'll make a profit in the third year, and we got to work.

At this point we were still operating out of our little 1,200-square-foot office. The on-site staff consisted of

George, me, and a high school kid who worked after school to help me package orders. (Bryan Stein was around, but his focus was IT.) Because money was so tight, everyone wore all the hats. Part of my official duties included driving our high school employee home every night so he wouldn't have to take the bus alone. Miriam was busy being a mom, but she still helped out most every day, and my parents pitched in, too. Our little skeleton crew answered the phones, took orders, filled bottles by hand, labeled them, packaged them, and shipped them. We swept the floors and took out the garbage. When a big order came in, we created our own assembly line in the warehouse: my father hand-filled bottles of monomer, my mother applied labels, and I closed the caps. The building had no air conditioning, and it was so hot my dad's "uniform" consisted of nothing more than his swim trunks.

When we didn't have something, we made do. For example, we did not own a machine to cover orders in protective shrink wrap because we couldn't afford one. So we bought industrial-sized rolls of shrink wrap, wound it around orders ourselves, and then put them in the sun and waited for the heat to naturally shrink the wrap. That was a four- or five-hour process, during which we prayed it wouldn't rain. Courtesy of divine intervention or Southern California's year-round good weather, we came out okay.

These were the days of learning on the go, making decisions on the fly, improvising, and doing many different jobs simultaneously. George and I were routinely putting in twelve-hour days and sometimes more, and by then we were also beginning to log plenty of hours on the road to promote OPI at trade shows.

Inevitably, there were mistakes along the way. At first I had no idea how to fill out purchase orders, so I simply slapped on the date I ordered something . . . which resulted in chaos when I made several orders on the same day and no one could identify the right order. Then when it came time to pay our sales rep his first commission check—for the whopping sum of $36—the check bounced because I hadn't deposited enough to cover the fees for opening a new account. I suppose my bad luck with anything involving payroll never left me! Thankfully this rep stuck with us because we had such a solid relationship, and later, we had that returned check framed.

So, bit by bit, with countless hours of hard work, we built the business and established ourselves in the western United States. Then just as we were managing to break even, the sales repping firm came to us and said if we wanted to keep growing, we needed to offer more than a single product. So we went back to the drawing board and decided to make the best-quality ancillary products, too—nail polish removers, nail forms, brushes, files. Anything the professional nail tech needed to perform the service, we'd provide something better than what was currently available.

And once *those* products were selling well, it was time to expand. Because of all the buzz around OPI as well as our reputation in the industry as good people with a good product, sales repping firms began contacting us and asking to represent us. So we expanded bit by bit over the next few years, hiring reps in the Northeast, then the Midwest, and then the South, until we had a presence in all fifty states. We moved into a bigger building so we'd have more room to store inventory.

Now George and I were working more than ever as everything was happening so quickly, and we were on the road at even more trade shows, in even more states. We knew we were putting everything into OPI, but the reputation of the brand was growing beyond our wildest expectations. OPI had become the new buzzword in beauty, and not just at salons in all fifty states but at beauty and vocational schools. Because we'd carefully established ourselves as *the* brand for salon professionals, anyone who offered courses for certification in nail services used OPI.

With all of this buzz, OPI grew by leaps and bounds. Even with more employees—we were up to fifteen or twenty by then—we could barely keep up with demand, and we were all practically run off our feet working.

But the result was undeniable: by 1987, OPI was the number-one professional salon brand in America. Naturally we were proud of this extraordinary accomplishment, but we didn't stop to celebrate. We couldn't! Our days were filled with meeting customer demand and just trying to stay on top of OPI's rapid expansion.

Yet even in the midst of the fray, I was already dreaming of the next big thing, of innovations not only in our products but with the very way the nail care industry operated. I was convinced I saw a need that no one else had. It was time to make a move. A big, bold move that would shake things up. Permanently.

three

TOUCAN DO IT IF YOU TRY

I HAVE A VIVID MEMORY OF A SCENE THAT TOOK PLACE IN Hungary when I was a little girl of seven. My family and some of my parents' friends were visiting Lake Balaton. Everyone was laughing and talking by the water, and I marched up to my mom and announced that I'd like to *tupirozni* her hair. The whole crowd laughed in amazement—how did a child of seven know about teased hair? This was the era of enormous bouffant hairstyles, which I must have seen on television. Someone fetched a comb, and my very patient mother let me go to work. When I was done, her hair reached for the sky. Though it was obvious I was never going to be a hairdresser, I now think of that day as my first foray into the world of beauty.

I really can't remember a time when I wasn't acutely aware of beauty in any form—color, art, architecture, nature, fashion. It was like I had a heightened sensitivity to visual instances of beauty, and this was especially the case for color.

So, in 1987 when George and I decided our next phase of expansion would be to enter the world of nail color, I felt I had a very good eye and keen instincts. And when I looked out and surveyed the lay of the land at the time, it struck me that a thorough makeover of the nail care category was long overdue. The handful of nail polishes on the market had generic, utilitarian names like Red No. 4, Mauve No. 3, and Pink No. 2, and the only people getting professional manicures on a regular basis were celebrities. Most women had never visited a nail salon, and the few who had went only for very special occasions, such as a wedding or a holiday party.

To put it simply, I saw that the nail care category had missed the mark when it came to its own consumers. It had failed to connect with women on an emotional level. It didn't offer them anything relevant to their lives; it didn't offer them anything exciting or personal. But I knew that women loved things that made them feel good—things like color, glamour, travel, and food. And they love to change their look. The industry was missing a huge opportunity in not establishing an emotional connection to its own consumers. Most women had no idea what nail color could do for them and how empowering it could be because the industry had never communicated that message.

And perhaps that was because the industry had missed the memo, too.

It's worth wondering if part of the disconnect was occurring because so many of the people running the industry at the time were men. I'm not here to cast blame or play Monday morning quarterback with an industry that was very, very good to me. But I do think there were marketing messages that simply didn't occur to men, nor did it occur to them to try to establish an emotional connection between their products and their buyers. But as a woman myself who had the same beauty goals and needs as our customers, these were among my first goals. This is one of the many reasons it's so important for women to be in leadership positions in business. Women's perspectives are invaluable, especially in industries that largely cater to female consumers, such as beauty. We instinctively know what women want, how to connect with them, and how to keep the connection going.

Back in the '80s most women had no idea how empowering nail color could be because the industry had never told them. OPI set out to permanently change the message of nails and give women a vast array of colors worthy of their STRENGTH AND POTENTIAL.

For me, nail color was never "just" nail polish, never a frivolous indulgence. Not even close. On the contrary, I saw nail color as a powerful means by which a woman could express herself—her individuality, her moods, her evolving styles, her beauty aspirations. It could also change not just her look but her entire outlook, and it could do so quickly and affordably. Need a spark of color to lift your spirits and ignite your passions? A lush purple could do that. Want to feel girly and fun? Try a high-shine pink. Or what if you're planning a night on the town and want to feel like a star? A vampy, gleaming red telegraphs Hollywood glamour. In my mind's eye, I saw a color for every mood and occasion.

So the first thing I would bring to the world of nail color was a vastly expanded palette. I'd give women a richer, broader, bolder language to work with. I'd give them the ability to communicate anything they wanted right there at their fingertips, on the world's smallest yet most powerful canvases.

Not So Bora-Bora-ing Pink

George and I got to work. Our first task was to scrupulously study the entire nail care category. Even though we had a good handle on the distribution side and the professional salon side, we revisited those aspects of the category, and now we made a thorough study of the consumer side, too. We knew that what was available to consumers was an inferior-quality product. But once we studied what our competitors were doing, we quickly realized that the cost of making the kind of product we wanted—the richest pigments, the highest-quality ingredients—wouldn't cost much more than what our competitors were paying for a subpar product. There was one problem solved!

With a good handle on financials, distribution, and salons, we focused our energies on the consumer. We decided that the biggest thing we wanted to gain was the loyalty of the consumer. On the top of our blackboard George wrote GAIN CONSUMER LOYALTY in giant letters, and this became our charge, our rallying cry, our organizing principle. How would we do that? By making nail color personal. We were entering an already-existing industry, after all, and about to revamp a product that had been around in China since as early as 3000 BC! So we were looking at how we could really shake things up, make things new and different.

Though this was years before "disruption" was a business buzzword, that was our intent from the beginning. We wanted the OPI debut collection to be totally unprecedented, and we wanted to completely rebrand the category of nail color. We agreed that it would be a serious misstep to come across in any way as dabblers—"like being a little bit pregnant," George said. To that end, we decided we'd hit the market with thirty shades. A full-color palette would signal that we were serious about the color business and here to stay. It would also allow me to create and present a full range of colors, everything from pure bright white to bold, inky burgundy.

But before we went to the drafting table or into the lab, we began with a change to the language. Instead of polish, we'd create a line of *lacquers*. "OPI Nail Lacquer" would not only differentiate our product from everything else on the market, it would help to elevate the entire experience of nail color. "Lacquer," with its rich pigmentation and amazing high-gloss shine, carried an aura of elegance, luxury, and, with its Indo-European roots, a whiff of glamour and travel—everything we wanted OPI to be about.

When it was time to create and test prototypes, George and I knew to divide and conquer. He and I are both very driven, Type-A personalities, with an obsessive attention to detail. One of the reasons we were able to work in the same small office for so many years without strangling each other is very simple: George did his thing and I did mine. It's one of the secrets to our success that cannot be underestimated.

One of the most important pieces of advice I give young people and budding entrepreneurs is to have a partner—a smart one, one you can trust to do their bit. I've always said that building a brand is like being in love—it takes an irrational devotion and a willing partner. When you're launching a business or rebranding a category, it's too difficult to do it all alone, and two partners can complement each other's strengths and make up for each other's weaknesses. Two people who can do the same thing very well may be one too many. But two

> *BUILDING A BRAND IS LIKE BEING IN LOVE. It takes an irrational devotion and a willing partner.*

people using their respective skills and working together for a common cause have the strength of many.

In our case, George was adept at infrastructure, design, and sales. He's the mastermind of The Big Idea—he could see the whole picture all at once, and he'd say, "This is what we're gonna do," and we'd do it. My strengths lay in anything involving the creative aspects—the colors, the trends, the marketing and advertising strategies, the creative team. With the debut line, George focused on designing the hardware while I was in charge of anything involving the lacquers, from identifying the hottest upcoming color trends to going into the lab with a colorist to develop them. We really couldn't have built OPI without each other.

We planned every single element down to the smallest detail, and we came up with an ergonomic design based on the professional nail technician's needs. The technician would be using the lacquers dozens of times a day, after all, and the bottle and the cap had to fit easily between her fingers and have the perfect weight and size. Likewise the brush had to be perfect, allowing a smooth, even flow of color and a precise application. The lacquer's consistency had to be exactly right so it would go on smoothly, without streaking, and most important, the color had to be highly pigmented so its full luster was evident with just one or two coats. We also took into account the aesthetics of the bottle. The cap would be a sexy jet black, providing a stark contrast to the color in the bottle. The logo had to be in a font that was tasteful and elegant. And we wanted a bottle that would be instantly recognizable even in silhouette, that would look beautiful on its own and as part of a collection on display.

George and I never worried about how long the testing phase was taking. We were in agreement that we wouldn't go out with a collection until it was the best it could possibly be. When you are rebranding a category and modernizing a product that's been on the market for hundreds of years, it's this attention to detail that separates the good from the great. We felt we had one shot to get this right, just one, and it had to be great.

The Color That Keeps on Giving

For color inspiration, I looked at trend prediction books from Paris and Milan to get a sense of the next big things happening in color, fashion, design, and culture in general. I wanted to see emerging trends happening across multiple aspects of society because I wanted to draw from the totality of cultural artifacts and give women colors that were relevant to their overall experience. I'm sure this omnivorous survey of color trends is something I'd be up to even if I didn't create for OPI—I've always been hyperaware of color all around me and of the way it affects people's moods. Now it was time to find the most beautiful and uplifting colors in the world and bring them to women.

But as they say, a successful endeavor is 10 percent inspiration, 90 percent perspiration. Back in 1987, no matter how inspired or excited I felt, I had no training in how to make nail lacquer and no notion of how to actually reproduce the colors I envisioned in my mind. So I relied on what had always worked for me—a clear long-range vision and a strong work ethic. Any time I wasn't on the road promoting OPI, I was spending anywhere from eight to twelve hours a day in the lab working side by side with an amazing colorist. Over the next year and a half, we produced and tested some eighty to ninety shades, and heaven only knows how many times we refined and improved the basic formula.

This was something of a trying period in the history of OPI. George is not a patient person and he wanted the line ready yesterday; I *am* a patient person but even to me the development phase seemed to be taking forever—and we were still busy running the dental business at the same time. I remember George and I had many yelling matches in Hungarian.

But we did agree on a 360-degree approach to operations and making money, which meant being thorough with the testing phase, the concept, the marketing, the sales team, the distribution, and the way we operated professionally. We also agreed, very crucially, that everything about the debut collection had to be perfect because we got only one chance to do this right. How we went out the door would affect our planning and how the brand grew for years to come. So George and I dug in and stayed focused, even through the fighting.

It probably didn't help that I was always painting his nails. Much of the nail color testing, of course, involved applying the lacquers to real nails. Many companies rely on plastic replicas, but I always liked to use natural nails to see how each and every aspect of the lacquer performed. We were examining not just its vibrancy and pigmentation and shine but its durability, consistency, flow, and drying time.

As we were still short on both money and time, my test subjects were anyone I could corner at the office. Most often that was George, Bryan Stein, and myself, as the three of us practically lived at OPI. Bryan was my favorite victim because he had very wide nail beds, which made it easy to see and examine the color. He would sigh when he saw me approaching with a tray of bottles, but he never said no—probably because he was too afraid! I was driven to obsession. After I'd examined his nails Bryan removed his color right away, but for George it was a different story. George routinely sported ten different colors on all ten of his nails, and he'd wear them proudly wherever he went—trade shows, sales meetings, restaurants.

Poor, beleaguered Bryan, meanwhile, claimed he couldn't get any work done because I was always giving him manicures. His opinion on the colors became a running joke. If he took a look and said, "I hate it," I said, "Good!" because I knew I'd struck gold.

Who Comes Up with These Names?

Finally, after nearly two years of intensive development and testing, we narrowed the lacquers down to the best of the best, the final thirty. And then it was time to name them. By far the most frequently asked question I've received over the years is, "Who comes up with those names?" Running a close second is the question's close cousin: "*How* do you come up with those names?"

I'll answer both, and I'll start at the beginning. For the debut collection, the names came about during a marathon brainstorming session between George, a brand manager named Judy Stonefield, and me. Armed with water, snacks, pads of paper, and pens, we literally locked ourselves in a little spare office and didn't come out until we had thirty names we all loved.

After thousands of colors and many dozens of collections, our naming sessions still follow this basic template. As OPI grew, we eventually moved into a large conference room, and sometimes there were as many as six people in attendance, but George and I were always there. One of the very best at OPI lacquer names was a purchasing agent named Susan Pfeffer. She worked for OPI for eighteen years and came up with some of our most memorable monikers. Fee Fi Fo Plum, I Have a Herring Problem, At Your Quebec and Call, Have a Tempura Tantrum, and Be There in a Prosecco are all brainchildren of Susan.

As a rule there is never any alcohol at our naming meetings, though there is plenty of coffee, sparkling water, and food. If we're creating names for a destination collection, we serve food from that country or region, and we decorate the room to match the theme. But otherwise we surround ourselves with stacks of trend books, color swatches, and fabrics for inspiration. We brainstorm for hours, generate hundreds of names, crack jokes that become increasingly risqué as the hours wear on, laugh to the point of tears, make multiple lists, narrow down, laugh some more, and then cast votes. These meetings are always the craziest and silliest times at OPI. The winning names are selected by democratic process, and the results are top secret: no one reveals even a hint of the names until we launch them to the public.

Plenty of times, names have occurred to me ahead of the meetings, but I do still put them up for a vote. To the best of my recollection they've all made it through. Up the Amazon Without a Paddle, OPI Red, Kyoto Pearl, My Address Is "Hollywood," Princesses Rule, Grand Canyon Sunset, Budapest Paprika, Mother Road Rose, NYPD Beet, Bet It All on OPI, Calling All Goddesses, and one of my personal favorites, My Dogsled Is a Hybrid, were all names I brought to the table. One name, It's a Wrap, came about by accident when near the end of a naming session I'd hit a wall and said, "Okay, I'm exhausted, it's a wrap." Everyone loved it as a lacquer name and voilà, we had our final name for the collection.

EVERY OPI LACQUER NAME COMES WITH A FANTASY and a cue for how to interpret that color.

So that's the actual *mechanics* of who comes up with our quirky, punny names and how we do it, but many OPI fans also want to know about the inspiration and the general philosophy behind them. To me this is one of the most beautiful aspects of OPI, and it helps explain how we were able to so quickly rebrand the entire nail care category. Every OPI lacquer name offers a cue for how to interpret the color. More specifically, every bottle of OPI Nail Lacquer comes with a little story that engenders a fantasy connected with that color.

Take Kyoto Pearl, for instance. This shade is near and dear to my heart because it's my mother's favorite. I wore it at my own wedding.

I knew from the beginning that I wanted a pearly white in the debut collection. In the spirit of OPI, however, it couldn't be just any white, and it couldn't even be the best white on the market. It needed a story and a fantasy as well, something that would reach out and connect to women on an emotional level and transport them to a place worthy of fantasy—and that's where the name came in.

So, instead of OPI White No. 1, or even OPI Pearly White No. 1, I created a pearl of a white, set in glamorous Kyoto. "Kyoto Pearl" connotes luxury, uniqueness, and a singular, rare beauty that arises through adversity. Right away, the consumer relates this lacquer to a precious pearl necklace. But it's also *Kyoto* Pearl, which instantly transports one to the land of exquisite temples, bamboo forests, blushing cherry blossoms, and delicious traditional cuisine.

The same went for the other lacquers in the debut collection. I didn't give women pink—I gave them a tasty, delicate cotton-candy shade of pink set in fun-filled Coney Island. I didn't give women a dark red—I gave them a glass of rich, aromatic wine they could only get in Malaga, Spain. Apparently our intentions resonated deeply with customers, as each of these colors—Kyoto Pearl, Coney

Island Cotton Candy, and Malaga Wine—proved so popular they're still on our list.

We knew the names would grab people's attention and make them laugh, but we had no idea how important they would be in rebranding the category, or how big a role they'd play in building the very DNA of OPI. The lacquers' names instantly set us apart from every other company and product out there. Red No. 4 and Pink No. 3 are easily lost in the shuffle, but just imagine the double takes that Alpine Snow, Swedish Nude, French Cognac, Cancun Fiesta, and Montreal Mauve provoked, and how memorable and curiosity-provoking they were. Everyone wanted to know more about the new line of nail lacquers with the crazy names.

That curiosity never faded. People all over the world now use OPI lacquer names in their own creative ways. Lacquer names have appeared in songs, novels, articles, blogs, television shows, and movies. People have made T-shirts and sweatshirts and posters with OPI names, Nicki Minaj has rapped about OPI in her hit "Make Me Proud," and Ellen Degeneres wrote and performed a poem about several of her favorites in one of her opening monologues before breaking into dance:

> *Roses are Pretty and Privileged,*
> *Violets are Escape to Bahama,*
> *Blue is Got a Date To-Knight,*
> *Perfect for my Mama.*
> *The grass is uncommitted,*
> *The sun is Goldilocks Rocks!*

My toes are Clubbing Til Sunrise,
Though I go to bed at 8 o'clock.
The moon is All Lacquered Up,
The stars are Tickle My France-y,
Now that you've learned all these colors,
It's time for me to dance-y.

People get engaged with the help of OPI lacquers like Mimosas for Mr. and Mrs.; they throw themed parties based on lacquers such as Chick Flick Cherry, 20 Candles on My Cake, Underneath the Mistletoe, and Met on the Internet; they use lacquers to announce that they're pregnant or that they've given birth (It's a Boy! It's a Girl!). If there is an occasion in life to be remembered or celebrated, there is an OPI lacquer for it.

All those crazy, quirky names really put us in a category all of our own and are an enduring hallmark of the brand. We never took ourselves too seriously, and part of our overall vision was that we wanted to make people happy. The lacquer names inevitably bring a smile to people's faces. I'm sure many OPI fans look forward to the new names as much as they look forward to the new colors.

I Cannoli Wear OPI

Once we released the debut collection in the autumn of 1989, reactions started to come in almost immediately. The first feedback was from the salon owners and nail technicians. When clients entered the salon, they encountered a 360-degree display featuring all thirty lacquers. It was a visually arresting sight, showcasing the vibrancy of the colors and an unprecedented range of choices, and it created buzz all on its own. Salon owners found their clients drawn immediately to the OPI line, and after they checked out the colors and heard the attention-grabbing names, they were convinced to give it a try. Then they loved the quality and the look of the lacquers on their nails, and they came back for more.

Salon owners and clients alike also loved the OPI color chart. This was another OPI innovation. The color chart showed the consumer all of the OPI shades that were available. It was small enough that a client could drop it in her purse and take it home—where she could start dreaming about the color she'd choose for her next manicure. Salon owners credited the chart with increasing their bookings. This thrilled us because we'd created the line with the professional in mind. We wanted to bring prestige and professionalism to the entire industry, and we wanted to increase earnings for the workers on the front lines, the nail techs and the salon owners. Quite quickly, salons were getting more calls from women asking for OPI or for individual OPI lacquers, many of them laughing as they wondered if the salon carried this new color they'd heard about called Swedish Nude. Many clients were women who were drawn in by all the buzz and were getting manicures for the first time—and after they loved the results, they kept coming back. This is a businessperson's dream come true. We were pulling the customer into the salon to ask for the brand by name, and we were pushing her out the door with such a good experience that she felt compelled to tell her friends about it.

Then we heard from the distributors and the sales reps, who told us everyone was going crazy for the collection and demand was like nothing they'd ever seen. As the buzz increased, George and I held additional sales meetings with our distributors and attended more trade shows. Held over three days at convention centers, trade shows were an opportunity for representatives from all the branches of beauty—hair, skin, nails, fragrance—to showcase and sell products. As many as thirty thousand people would attend in order to buy new products and be the first to see emerging trends. After the debut collection was such a hit,

> *If you're designing something new or revamping a category, CREATE A PRODUCT THAT SPEAKS FOR ITSELF—and that consumers can't stop talking about.*

George and I watched heads turn and we heard whispers of "Look, OPI is here" when we entered the room at trade shows. This was mind-blowing stuff for two poor kids from Hungary, but we figured we were enjoying our fifteen minutes of fame, and we stayed focused on the work.

What was truly remarkable was how quickly the word traveled. Obviously this was years before the Internet, but it was also before we had a PR campaign and before we were advertising in fashion and beauty magazines. The fact was, the collection spoke for itself. With the whole package—the design, the quality, the colors, the names, the fun, the excitement—OPI debuted in a class all its own.

But we were operating in the world of beauty and fashion, and that world never rests. Consumers always want the next big thing. So, even as we were enjoying the game-changing success of our launch, we were already at work on the next collection. We wanted a permanent place in the industry, and remaining relevant in the beauty industry requires that you continually innovate so you can continually excite and surprise and delight the consumer. You must stay on top of trends and get the jump on them before anyone else does.

Alternatively, you can *create* the trends yourself. You can establish yourself as an industry tastemaker and influencer, and that's what we set out to do with our next phase of development.

We would create the trends, not follow them.

four

COLOR SO HOT IT BERNS

THIS ERA OF OPI'S HISTORY WAS INCREDIBLY EXCITING, but what wasn't visible to the public was all the long hours we were putting in behind the scenes. This is surely the case for all branches of the beauty and fashion industries—the public sees the glossy spreads and the runway shows, but they are the end result of many hours of labor by many people. In our case, the next phase of development always meant another collection. Like any product-driven business, we had to expand our line in order to gain broader market share. And now we had a growing legion of fans who were eager to see what we would come up with next.

Because we were still such a small staff, preparing and releasing the next collection required all hands on deck, seven days a week. And as we didn't yet own industrial-sized equipment, we were still doing much of the work the old-fashioned way. I have vivid memories of many nights of filling bottle after bottle of lacquer by hand until 10 or 11 at night. George had a family of four by now—his daughter Nicole had arrived in 1985—and went home at a decent hour to be with them, while I was still single and could work around the clock if need be. This kind of work was just as boring and monotonous as my former days of packing shirts at the factory in New York, and sometimes I just wanted to cry. There I was by myself in a warehouse late at night, I hadn't eaten in hours, and I was too scared to go out. Alone in the dark with so much work to do, my thoughts took a dark turn. *Why am I not in New York? Why am I not out with some cute guy? And my God, I'm* **starving***. I haven't even had time to grab a granola bar, and I've been standing for* **hours***, and everything aches, and oh my God what if this next line is a total flop?*

It was right about then, tears about to spill, that I'd check myself. I knew no good could come of succumbing to a downward spiral of self-pity. I tell my audiences of young people and aspiring entrepreneurs that they can't allow themselves to get lost in their own heads like that—believe me, I know. If you want to indulge in a *little* self-pity, that's fine, but at some point you've got to shake yourself out of it.

To get myself out of those low moments, I remembered where I came from, and I reminded myself that I did not want to go back there. The only real option was to go forward, and the only way to do that was to stick it out . . . just a little more . . . and a little more after that. Standing there in the lonely warehouse, famished and my back and arms aching from filling bottles, I made myself envision the finish line—how beautiful

When you find yourself discouraged, THINK of your customers. VISUALIZE how thrilled they'll be with your next product—and then GIVE them the product that will elicit that kind of reaction.

the next collection would be, and how eagerly our customers were awaiting it. It's always a fantastic motivator to keep thinking of your customers. Picture them over the moon with the next product—and then give them the product that will elicit that kind of reaction. Then I took a deep breath and filled and sealed another bottle—and I rejoiced each time I reached a new milestone. Another dozen bottles, another box filled and sealed.

For our second collection and every one thereafter, we decided to present a dozen lacquers. We'd wanted to go big with our debut and show a wider variety of colors than anyone had ever seen, but from that point onward, we'd streamline to a tidy twelve. There were two basic reasons for this. One was an ultra-practical marketing decision: twelve shades were easy to package and ship, and it was easy to do promotions based upon a dozen lacquers. But more importantly, we decided to take a cue from the fashion industry and release seasonal collections, which would require quick production. Though we were creating and selling a beauty product, we considered ourselves part of the larger fashion industry, with a product that was as integral to completing a look as the latest runway styles and the perfect makeup. The fashion industry was all about colors and trends, and OPI was, too. This was all part of my vision of making nail color not just another beauty product but a must-have fashion accessory, as essential to completing a look as hair or makeup or the perfect pair of shoes.

For our second collection I again scanned the globe for places that would transport women to their fantasy travel destinations, and I gave them colors from Paris, Rome, L.A., and the Tropics. These were warm-weather hues, invoking a spirit of fun in the sun, island-hopping, and luxury travel. Among the shades from this collection were lacquers such as Caribbean Coral, Spanish Almond, Florida Flamingo, and Tropical Punch. We released this Spring/Summer collection in March 1990, but well before it arrived in salons, I was already at work on the Fall/Winter 1990 collection. That one followed a similar international theme, with lacquers such as Bar-berry Coast, St. Louis Cardinal, Tuscany Terra Cotta, and Peruvian Persimmon making an appearance. This collection also featured a lacquer that would turn out to be among the most beloved OPI shades of all time. Cajun Shrimp, a rich, spicy coral, was such a hit that it's never left the color chart.

So this is how it would go. I could see my future stretching out before me, my life's work a cycle of dreaming up, creating, presenting, and promoting seasonal lacquer collections. I assumed that at some point we would ramp up production and release more collections per year, but already, all signs said we'd be in the color business for the long term, just as we'd intended.

In the meantime, I had to eat. Every day around 3 p.m. I'd start to become faint from hunger, as there was never enough time for a proper lunch. My salvation arrived in the form of an employee named Marcello Ruano, whom I called Mar-*chel*-lo after heartthrob Italian actor Marcello Mastroianni. Marcello was one of OPI's early employees, and he worked in the factory to help fill bottles. One day around 3 in the afternoon he found me slumped at my desk, overcome with fatigue and hunger. He ran back to the breakroom and returned with his lunch leftovers— which I gratefully gobbled up and declared the best thing I'd ever eaten. The next day, I just *happened* to drift by his station around the same time, and again, Marcello shared his food. You can see where this is going. I suspect Marcello started packing extra in his lunch box, because he knew whenever I was in the building I'd be dropping by around midafternoon. Marcello worked with us for thirty years. In no small part, we have kind Mar-*chel*-lo to thank for getting all those collections out the door.

Two-Timing the Zones

As you have no doubt already gathered, food has always been an important part of my life and George's. We both love to eat, and we love to cook (though if I had to choose one it would be eating). George and I also both love to travel and explore the world, so it was inevitable that food and travel were woven into the DNA of the OPI brand from the very beginning. They were our primary inspirations, and they were what we knew best.

At first glance that may seem crazy—what do food and travel have to do with nail color?—but they're not at all as far apart as they seem. To us they were two of life's primary pleasures, and from the beginning we wanted to take the consumer along with us on a beautiful journey. What better way to connect with consumers on a personal level than to take them around the globe with us on travel and culinary adventures?

> *FOOD and TRAVEL are two of life's primary pleasures, and we wove them into the DNA of OPI from the very beginning.*

The theme of the journey—of getting away from it all, of being spirited away to a beautiful, exciting place—just made intuitive sense to me. Let's face it—every woman on the planet has had fantasies of escaping her everyday life. For most of us, deeply engaged in the throes of work and family and community, actual island-hopping or nightly fine dining just isn't possible. But what OPI *could* do was give every woman a little bit of luxury, a taste of another place. We could give her a bit of color and personal attention to brighten her day. With a small bottle of nail lacquer, we could bring the world to women's fingertips by taking them to places they dreamt of.

All that in a half-ounce bottle of lacquer, you say? Absolutely! If you think about it, the salon experience itself is a mini-getaway, a peaceful oasis in the midst of a busy life. You're not answering emails or waiting in the carpool line or tidying up or attending meetings. When you don't have the opportunity to get away, you can still pop into the salon for a time that's just for you, and you can do this quickly and affordably, without compromising your schedule or your pocketbook.

The personal touch you receive at the salon is also so important. There is no other beauty service where you're sitting face-to-face with your service provider. With hair, the stylist is most often behind you, and regular professional makeup applications just aren't feasible for most women. But at the nail salon, you relax in a comfy chair while a skilled professional takes your hands in hers. It's an intimate experience, one of relaxation and physical touch and personal attention. I've often thought of it as its own form of psychoanalysis. You leave the salon refreshed and relaxed, looking and feeling better. So, you see, while the nail color is the medium, what OPI was really offering was an entire experience.

A professional manicure also provides instant gratification. I made sure to create a color for every mood and beauty aspiration, and once it's applied, your whole look is transformed and you've got an accessible means of happiness right there at your fingertips. Any time you need a little pick-me-up, all you have to do is look at your hands. As far as beauty services go, nails are the one thing that doesn't require you to get up and go to a mirror to check out and enjoy. You can simply glance at your hands as you type, as you text, as you pick up kids or zip a zipper, to get a taste of the beautiful color you chose and receive a little spark of joy and confidence.

Our vision to bring consumers with us on a journey around the world grew stronger with each new collection, and when PR expert Harris Shepard joined our team in 1991, he immediately understood what we were about. With his guidance we clarified and solidified our vision, and I began to create collections that centered on a specific theme or destination. Thus the next one was 1991's Carnival Collection, which brought women high-energy, popping colors with a fun-filled theme. This is where the world was introduced to the likes of Chinese Firecracker, San Paolo Pink, New Orleans Mardis Gras, and Pamplona Peach. Next up was our first dedicated destination collection—the International Collection—which took women from Italy to Nova Scotia, from Persia to Polynesia, from South Korea to Vienna, and beyond. The following year we released two more seasonal collections, and then starting in 1993, we shifted our focus to specific destinations. It began with Deer Valley, moved on to the Mediterranean and then Scandinavia, then America and the Winter Resort collection. We've now taken our customers to all corners of the globe, from Japan to Fiji, from the South Seas to South America, from Vegas to Australia, from Canada to the Caribbean, from Russia to the Painted Desert, from India to Iceland . . . There are far too many to name!

Promoting OPI has taken us all over the world as well. Again, George and I divided and conquered: he took all of Asia, and I traveled throughout North America, Latin America, and Europe. Once when traveling overseas, a passport officer asked me the routine question of the purpose of my visit. I told her I was going to a PR event for OPI nails, and suddenly she was up out of her seat and coming around to me. Instantly I was having flashbacks to Hungary and my heart leapt—was I being detained? But no, she was presenting her nails. "Look, look!" she exclaimed. "I'm wearing OPI!" I hugged her out of sheer relief and gratitude.

People often ask me if I have a favorite collection— either for the colors or because promoting it took me to some favorite destination. Well the truth is, I do! My two favorites are the New York City collection from 2000 and the Italian collection from 2001. How could I not fall for those? New York City was the first place I came to in America, and it was the city that welcomed my family and gave us freedom and a better life. Big Apple Red was a standout from that collection and remains one of my personal favorites. Fans apparently feel the same way, as it's been one of our all-time bestsellers.

And Italy . . . well, does anything more need to be said? What's not to love about beautiful Italy, one of the most gorgeous countries on earth, with its perfect Mediterranean climate, its warm people, its culture, and of course, its world-class food? Plus who hasn't fantasized about some handsome Italian? Italian Love Affair was one of my favorites from that collection; it's a pale, peachy pink with just a hint of a shimmery finish. It telegraphs romance and the first intoxicating blush of love. Madonna wore this lacquer when she married Guy Ritchie. But I also can't fail to mention a bright, orangey-red lacquer from this collection with one of my favorite names of all time: Hey Vito, Is My Car Red-y? All these years later it still makes me laugh—and I'm not the only one who loves it. A New Jersey–based auto mechanic named Vito used to buy this color in bulk to give to his customers. I wish I could take credit for that name, but that goes to brand manager Judy Stonefield. Well done, Judy.

> *Italian Love Affair is one of my favorite colors. It's a pale, peachy pink that telegraphs the FIRST INTOXICATING BLUSH OF LOVE. Madonna wore it when she married Guy Ritchie.*

Made Your Look

With every new collection the hype and the buzz and the customer anticipation grew, and that multiplied by orders of magnitude once Harris took over PR for OPI. As you'll recall, I didn't even know what "pee-are" was when George and I met Harris, but I was a quick learner. As we were now creating products not just for salon professionals but for the individual consumer, Harris led us into an all-new way of reaching our customers—one that would change the way beauty advertising was done.

By this time we were beginning to turn a modest profit, but we still couldn't afford to buy advertising in the glossy fashion magazines. The only paid advertising we'd done was small adverts in professional trade publications such as *NAILS Magazine* and *NAILPRO Magazine*. So, instead, Harris and I pursued the social media of our day, which was public relations. What that meant back then was that he and I spent a lot of hours traveling and meeting with a lot of beauty editors. Harris knew everyone in the business, so he was able to book all of our meetings. We were young and ambitious, and good thing, as the schedule we kept was insane. At least twice a year and often more, Harris and I would book a two- or three-day trip to New York City to meet with thirty or forty fashion and beauty editors from all the top magazines—*Glamour*, *Vogue*, *Allure*, *W*, *Marie Claire*, and so on. I'd present the latest collection, press bottles of lacquer into editors' hands, thank them, and then move right on to the next meeting. Though I was delivering largely the same pitch at each magazine, I was authentic and enthusiastic. I think this is key. People can see through inauthenticity in a heartbeat, and the second they do, you've lost your opportunity. On the other hand, authenticity endorses your product all on its own, and high-energy enthusiasm is contagious. My pitches made a personal connection to editors (once again, relationships are key), and then the quality of the product spoke for itself and sealed the deal.

Over the years, George and Harris and I made an effort to connect to many, many people in the fashion and beauty industries and to build relationships with them. In the days before the Internet and social media, promotion was a very personal encounter, and we put in a lot of hours, in person and on the phone. Though I was certainly the most reserved of the three of us, I was fearless when it came to promoting OPI. I'd cold call any editor and urge them to give OPI a try, and of course, I'd follow up by sending them samples. All of that work paid off. Because we put in that extra effort and made the personal connection, we always got a meeting. It's very interesting for me to see how marketing has changed over the years through the advent of social media—as well as how it's remained the same. The way we make connections is different, but the content of the meetings and their intended outcomes haven't changed at all.

What we were aiming for with all this groundwork was to be featured in the magazine. If the editors loved what they saw, they'd run an article on OPI or give us an editorial mention. If an editor wrote, for example, that Big Apple Red was the best red they'd seen in years, or The Thrill of Brazil was the hottest new color of the season, that

When you're just starting out and money is tight, leverage all your social media platforms to bring exposure to your business. FREE PRESS IS EVERY BIT AS GOOD AS PAID PRESS.

was pure advertising gold. And if they featured a photograph of the bottle or the color along with the copy, jackpot! I always tell people that if they're new to business or on a tight budget, they should do whatever they can to get free press—which is easier than ever through social media. Free press is every bit as good as paid press.

Eventually we did do paid advertisements in big fashion magazines. In 1993, Harris and George and I took a lunch meeting with a couple of executives from a new magazine that was still in the planning stages called *InStyle*. We liked what we heard, so, right then and there, George signed a five-year advertising deal on the back of a cocktail napkin. Our first full-page ad would appear in *InStyle*'s June 1994 inaugural issue—and as usual for OPI, it would be different from anything out there.

At that time there was very little advertising for nail care products, certainly not compared to makeup or hair, and beauty product ads appeared only in the back pages of fashion magazines. But we wanted OPI lacquers prominently featured, and we wanted an all-new type of ad. So Harris insisted that our ads be placed in the front pages of the magazines, and we made sure the model's hands were the main focus of the shot. Also for the first time, the ads included the name of the lacquer the model was wearing as well as the name of the nail technician who'd done the manicure. Everyone got credited, and listing a lacquer name such as Kissimmee Kiss or Chilly Chile only drew more attention to OPI and created more buzz. Our ads also included information on where to buy OPI lacquers, as well as how long that particular collection would be available—usually in the form of "available for a limited time" at independent salons and beauty supply stores, for example, which heightened urgency.

Another change Harris later instituted was the advertising strategy centered on "Suzi's Picks." Let's say we released a new collection in January. The media would cover it in January and maybe February, but what if we wanted more press and didn't want to wait until the next seasonal collection for it? That's where the idea of Suzi's Picks was born. I'd pick my top three favorites from each collection, and then the media would do a follow-up featuring those lacquers. So we'd end up getting twice the publicity for the same collection. Meanwhile, fashion and beauty editors always wanted fresh content, and Suzi's Picks delivered that. It was an easy means for publicity and a fun feature in magazines, so soon enough, editors began calling to ask for Suzi's Picks. Another beneficial partnership.

All of these changes—which today may seem commonplace or obvious—constituted an enormous transformation in the way beauty advertising was done. Harris says, without exaggeration, that we changed the face of beauty.

However you characterize it, it worked. After our new ad campaigns, consumer demand for OPI doubled and tripled and quadrupled, and it was up to me to keep producing new colors and collections, to keep exciting and surprising the consumer. We began hiring more employees to help. I told the sales force that they needed to go out and sell every collection like it was the first collection—they needed to maintain that level of excitement.

"And for my part," I said, "I'll create every collection like it's my first."

Word of OPI was making its way around the globe by then, so I was creating on a world stage. The stakes felt high—because they were.

Otherwise Engaged

With all the craziness of a rapidly expanding brand—the insane working hours, the frequent travel, and the constant demand for innovation—I'd never had time for a relationship. Oh I'd been on plenty of blind dates over the years—more than my fair share! Before online dating, people met at bars or dinner parties or some sort of public function, like a wedding or an art opening or a civic event. But especially among immigrants, many dates were orchestrated by family, usually your mother and her friends. (This is still the case, by the way. The most sophisticated online dating algorithms are no match for a motivated mama.) By the time OPI was releasing seasonal collections, I'd been on more blind dates than I care to recall.

Some, I really, really wish I could forget, like the guy who took me to a concert at Carnegie Hall. It was yet another date arranged by my mother and one of her Hungarian friends, and as usual, she had high hopes for a match. We were to meet at a certain corner. I arrived early and watched with sinking heart as all sorts of handsome men hurried by. Then at the appointed time I saw a terribly unattractive man shuffling toward me, and I thought, *Please, please, don't let that be him, don't let him call out my name.* That very second he started waving and screaming, "Zsuzsi! Zsuzsi Weiss! Is that you?!" at the top of his lungs. He turned out to be cheap and aggressively boring, too, so I did a terrible thing: at the concert I told him I had to go to the ladies' room, and I never went back. I took the subway home, and my mom was livid. Not just for my rudeness but because she could never again show her face to the friend who'd set us up, and no one would want to set me up for a while.

In any event, most of these blind dates weren't nearly this bad; they were just okay, and nothing had ever taken off. As you can imagine, as I reached my thirties and was still single, my deeply traditional parents were deeply concerned. They were worried not only that I was missing out on the joys of marriage and family but that I was married to my job.

The truth is, they were right! I spent nearly all of my waking hours working. OPI was a true passion for me, and to this day I still love going to work and feel restless on the weekends as I wait impatiently for Monday morning to arrive. I feel most uncomfortable when I'm supposed to be "relaxing" (I even detest that word), and most at home and most useful when I'm working. The busier I am, the better. But my family kept pestering, and kept arranging blind dates, which I'd go on out of duty . . . only to suffer the same outcome. Finally I couldn't take it anymore. "That's it!" I announced to the whole family. "No more blind dates!" And just to make sure they got the point, I followed up with, "I'm over it! I'm done! They're just one disaster after another."

So it wasn't my family who called in late 1990 with the offer of yet another blind date. It was my real estate agent. She had a client I just *had* to meet, a physician who, like me, had recently purchased a condo.

I agreed to meet George—yes, another George, this one George Fischmann—for dinner. We found that we had a lot in common and much to talk about. Like me George was an immigrant—he was born in Guatemala after his parents left Czechoslovakia during World War II—and he, too, came from a very traditional Jewish family. His father had passed away when he was two, but his mother still lived in Guatemala. George came to America as a young boy to attend a yeshiva in New York and then went to high school in Los Angeles because his sister lived there. Now he was a physician in a private practice, so he, too, had a very busy career. What's more, his family had owned a cosmetics business in Guatemala, so he had a great deal of respect for what I was doing and he understood how much work was required.

After dinner George asked if he could call me again and I said yes. As I remember it he called once, though George insists it was "several" times. Who knows where the truth lies! Whatever happened, we were both extremely busy, and for one reason or another we just didn't connect again. I shrugged and got back to work, chalking it up to yet another failed blind date.

Nearly a year later I ran into my real estate agent, who told me she'd recently seen George and asked him why he'd never called me back. George replied that he had, and that *I* was the one who'd never returned *his* call. Again, George and I are both sticking to our versions of the story. Whatever it was, the agent convinced him to give it another shot.

Sure enough, I heard from George the next day, and we went out to dinner again. This time something just clicked. We began seeing each other more frequently—

but not exclusively. George struck me as the eternal bachelor, in no hurry to settle down. As the months went on George and I continued to enjoy spending time together, but there was no sign of a commitment. My family grew more and more worried. "Zsuzsi," said my father, "I'm afraid you're chasing a train that isn't stopping."

By then it was August of 1991. George was thirty-six, and I was thirty-five. My dad had a point. If the relationship was never going to progress past the dating stage, it was time to move on. I suggested to George that we take a break.

George was taken aback—apparently he hadn't seen that coming at all. And apparently he didn't want to break up or even take a short break, because the next time we were at my family's house, just before Rosh Hashanah, he surprised us all by asking my father for my hand. My father looked at me quizzically—George wanted my *hand*? I leaned over and said in Hungarian, "Dad, this is it! He means he wants to get married."

The next few moments were right out of a movie. My parents jumped up and cheered, and my mom started crying. Everyone hugged and kissed, and it was an afternoon of celebration.

Then I didn't hear from my new fiancé for two whole days. He and his sister were getting ready for Rosh Hashanah and he was very observant, so for the next two days he did not drive in a car or talk on the phone. I figured he was praying in temples crying out, "What did I just do? What did I just do?"

But I suppose if he had any qualms he got over them, because the very second the new year's celebrations were complete, everyone threw themselves into wedding planning. My sister and George's sister led the charge—they were in full agreement that at our ages there wasn't a moment to lose. It was his sister who said we should get married that very year. So, on December 15, 1991, George and I married, and I became Suzi Weiss-Fischmann. Another new name for yet another evolution in my identity.

Even on such short notice, over three hundred people attended the wedding. I don't think anyone believed George Fischmann was ever going to get married.

— five —

WE THE FEMALE

O PI CONTINUED TO GROW RAPIDLY, BUT NOT WITHOUT OC-
casional stumbles. We experienced one of our biggest
setbacks in 1993 and 1994. The trend at the time was
for matching lip and nail color, and as OPI was an established success by then, distributors everywhere thought
we'd be a sure bet when we branched out into lip color.
We did, too.

· But in addition to not knowing the territory of lipstick as well as we should have, we did not own the equipment to create the product or fill the tubes, so we had

to outsource those tasks. At first, all was well. Quality control tests came back fine, and the first local shipments progressed without a problem. But when shipments started arriving at national distributors, the calls started coming in. Every tube of lipstick—and we're talking millions of them—had bloomed. Translation? Each lipstick emerged covered in tiny beads of condensation. They looked *terrible*, like they'd developed some sort of disease. Not a single tube could be salvaged, and we had to recall and discard the entire lot.

Which meant we lost millions of dollars. As we were still a growing business and still determined to make payroll, the loss threw us into financial turmoil. (I always said you don't actually own a business until you're making payroll and paying taxes. Until you're responsible for other people, you're just talking!) Our finances were already strained because we'd grown so rapidly, which had required expanded infrastructure, more equipment, and additional employees. These were all good problems to have, but few growing companies are prepared for the sudden loss of millions of dollars.

When we sat down to analyze what had gone wrong— surely one of the gloomiest OPI meetings on record— we concluded that we'd failed to correctly analyze our distribution channels. At that time, lipstick was sold mainly at two places: bargain lipstick at chain drugstores and supermarkets, and higher-end lipstick at fine department stores. OPI Nail Lacquer was sold mainly at salons, so the salon distribution channel was what we knew—but nail salons were not where women went to buy lipstick. Thus the brand-new product of OPI Lip Color required a whole new distribution channel—one that obviously we didn't know well enough. We'd also failed to take into account the

NEVER release a new product until you've researched every angle; NEVER sink money into an area you don't know well; and NEVER put your trust in another entity unless you know them inside and out.

effects of a summertime launch on the formula: the high temps sparked and accelerated the blooming process.

Lessons learned? Never release a new product until you've *thoroughly* done your homework; never sink so much money into an area that you don't know well; and never put your trust in another entity unless you know them well.

And if at all possible, avoid launching a lipstick line in the summer.

This setback did have one very positive outcome, however. As we never wanted to repeat such a mistake, one that could put our employees' livelihoods and OPI's reputation in jeopardy, we decided we'd stick to what we knew best, and that was nails. We refocused our efforts and redoubled our energies. It took more than a year, but we did recover our losses.

And good thing, because while all of this was occurring, huge changes were taking place in my personal life, every one of them requiring more and more of my attention at home.

It's a Girl! It's a Boy!

Marriage to George Fischmann was (and is) amazing. Our early days together were a constant back-and-forth between working and having fun, working and having fun. We both loved our jobs and gave them our best— and then when we were home we gave our best to family and friends. Most every day on my way home from work I'd buy fresh vegetables—a California luxury I still never take for granted—and I even attempted cooking. To this day George and I make a point to sit down and have dinner together every night we're not traveling. He was respectful enough to put up with my terrible cooking.

As were our friends—up to a point. George and I loved to entertain, and we loved to have people over for Friday night Shabbat dinner. The friends ate my food until they had a chance to taste my mother's cooking. And as our guest list grew and my meager cooking skills were strained to the point of breaking, our friends intervened and actually said, "Suzi, please don't do that." The majority of the cooking then fell to my mother, while I provided the house and the dinnerware and the fresh flowers. Meanwhile George was a wine connoisseur and paired my mother's exquisite dishes with beautiful wines. This arrangement made everyone—my mother, my father, George, our friends, and me—very happy.

Life proceeded in much this way until our daughter Andrea Rose was born in 1993. Our son Andrew David arrived in 1996. We were incredibly happy.

We were also incredibly busy.

So picture this: I have a newborn and a toddler, I'm co-running a company that's expanding into global markets, I'm dealing with the Great Lipstick Debacle, I'm traveling the world to promote OPI, and I'm creating at least four new lacquer collections a year. Now add into the mix that my husband has his own demanding job. And as we were a very traditional Jewish family, George rose at five every morning to pray, we hosted weekly Shabbat dinners (which certainly couldn't have happened without my mother's help), and we observed all the Jewish holidays and customs. If you think this sounds impossible, I can assure you that's exactly how it felt.

The life I led as a fully engaged family member *and* a business leader at the helm of a large company was completely crazy, and it's not one I would recommend for everybody. But it's the one I wanted. I'd do it all over again if given the choice.

I wouldn't have lasted one week, however, without a tremendous amount of help. I was very lucky to have my sister Miriam, my parents, and World's Best Dad George Fischmann, all of whom were more than willing to pitch in. Miriam, despite having a family of her own and working as an ambassador-at-large for OPI (she was forever making deliveries and showing around international distributors), was always available for my kids. I don't think there was a single orthodontist appointment that she didn't take them to. Our four children grew up together, and we all remain very close.

I also had the immense privilege of having my parents just minutes away. They read to Andrea and Andrew and took them to parks and taught them the traditions of our faith, and talked and sang to them in Hungarian. (Meanwhile, the kids learned Hebrew at Jewish day school, and George spoke to them in Spanish, so they got a real polyglot education.) And honestly, without my mother we probably would have starved. Cooking is her art, it is her passion, and it is how she expresses love. When my children were young she prepared dinner for us most every night, and the more people, the merrier. Miriam and her kids were often there, and Harris joined us from time to time as well. (My mother adores Harris and has a special fruit compote she prepares just for him. If he doesn't bring the empty jar back for a refill he gets reprimanded.)

My mom's Friday night Shabbat dinners were the highlight of everyone's week. She judged playdates by how much a kid ate and was baffled and worried when one of Andrea or Andrew's friends only picked at their food.

"But Mom," I'd say, "they probably just aren't hungry."

"Not possible!" she'd respond in Hungarian. "They must eat!"

Everyone was only too happy to have my mother cook. If for any reason she couldn't, we knew we were all in trouble. This was a time for takeout, and we had several local places on speed dial for just such emergencies.

And of course, there is simply no way I would have been able to remain so actively involved at OPI after we had children without a very understanding, very supportive husband. He was (and still is) an amazing husband and dad. George was always there to pick up the baton when

I had to travel or stay at work late. We were in full agreement that no matter how crazy work got, family came first. We were both the children of Holocaust survivors, both acutely aware of how much had been lost and how tenuous life could be. So we were firmly committed to putting family above all else, and this shared vision informed all of our decisions regarding family life and created an unshakable bond between us. The same went for our faith. It was very important to both of us to keep the traditions of our ancestors alive, and we raised the children in a traditional Jewish household. For many years OPI took me to far-flung places, but religious holidays and weekly Shabbat dinners always brought the family back together.

> *No matter how crazy work got, FAMILY ALWAYS CAME FIRST. George and I were the children of Holocaust survivors, acutely aware of how much had been lost and how tenuous life could be.*

As far as the day-to-day schedule went, we just did the best we could. Many days were catch-as-catch-can, with last-minute arrangements and George's or my scrambling to pick up or drop off a child. One of my greatest fears was that I wouldn't make it to carpool on time—and I admit that I was always the very last parent to arrive. I will also admit that there were even days the school traffic monitor had to knock on my window, as I'd fallen asleep in the carpool line. When I managed to stay awake, I made the most of my time and used the carpool moms as an impromptu focus group to test new colors. They eventually got used to my thrusting samples through their car windows and asking which they liked better, A or B.

Meanwhile, my children eventually got used to my tough-love attitude toward missing school: if a child wasn't actively vomiting or running a high fever they went to school, and if the nurse called, my first response was always to give the kid a couple of Tylenol and reassess in an hour or two. That was usually enough time to get them (by which I mean *me*) to the end of the school day.

Somehow or another, George and I made it work. No child was ever left behind. Not to the best of my recollection anyway.

I do strongly believe that for family and work life to coexist peacefully and fruitfully, *it has to begin at home*. It doesn't matter if you're running a large corporation from the corner office or a startup out of your basement—it's very important that you and your partner share a vision of family and of what you're willing to do to keep a household happy, a business running smoothly, and a relationship on solid ground. George understood from the very beginning that I was involved in building something entirely new and that it would demand much of my time. He knew how important family was

The old advice of NEVER GOING TO BED ANGRY is good advice—especially if you're trying to maintain a peaceful coexistence between work and family. The moment something seems wrong, address it, and always make time for your partner, even if it's a quick lunch or coffee date.

to me, but he also knew how important I felt it was to be in a marriage in which I was an equal partner. He was willing to play a larger role at home in order to give me more time to work.

In the meantime, we worked hard to find time for each other and to maintain open communication. The old advice of never going to bed angry is very good counsel. My husband and I never let anything fester. We were so busy that if we'd let even the smallest thing slide, the odds were extremely likely that it would never get resolved, and with enough old resentments accumulated, the relationship would not have lasted. So, even if it's a lunch or a coffee date, find time for your partner, and keep communication open. The minute something doesn't feel right, address it.

It does take a village to raise a child . . . especially if you're running a company. I'm very grateful that I did have a village, and they were the best of the best. With this kind of support system in place, I had the luxury of always knowing my children were safe and well cared for. So I may have faced guilt over being away, but I never faced worry.

The guilt, however, was formidable, and I struggled to let it go. I dealt with it in various ways, some more successful than others. A few times, I took the kids with me to trade shows that were close by. Those trips were okay, but in the end George and I concluded it wasn't the best choice. I faced more guilt over bringing them along and then not being able to spend time with them than I did over leaving them at home in the care of family, with their normal routines and friends. Which was better—a harried, stressed-out mom they saw in passing or a mother who could be fully present and available at home and during family vacations?

So what I resorted to was overscheduling myself every day I had to travel so I could get back home more quickly. Harris and I would hit multiple countries in a handful of days, and we did plenty of twenty-four-hour trips as well. Poor Harris! I admit I was a beast back then. Any time he wanted to enjoy a city or just slow down, I had one response: "We are not here to *play*, Harris, we are here to *work!*" We became accustomed to operating on two to three hours of sleep and expert at promptly dropping into unconsciousness the second we buckled into our airplane seats.

Sometimes Harris couldn't even wait that long. Once we were doing a multiple-city tour of Eastern Europe, and our last stop was Budapest. We were both exhausted, but I was so excited to be back in Budapest I was operating on adrenaline. I launched into a high-energy presentation, one of my best ever, only to look over and find Harris with his chin on his chest, snoring away in the front row. At other points it was I who was unable to function. Once, a Russian journalist was interviewing me near the end of a five-city tour of Europe, and I was so fatigued it took all my effort to keep my eyelids aloft, much less answer his questions. I lapsed into some sort of half-English half-Hungarian gibberish, and that's when Harris swooped in and got me out of there before I did further damage.

Thankfully, incidents like these were few and far between, and in fact, one of the reasons Harris and I worked so well together was that we shared a sense of urgency. We were supremely focused on growing OPI and willing to do whatever it took to promote the brand, including sacrificing sleep, leisure, and sometimes even peace of mind. There was a span of time when the kids were young, for example, that I was so busy and so wracked with guilt over missing out on time with them that I couldn't travel at all. I had always loved to travel and found flying exhilarating, but after the kids came along I actually began to have panic attacks on planes and even required oxygen a few times. I couldn't stop the litany of *what ifs* coursing through my mind. Harris got used to my canceling at the last minute after developing "mystery illnesses" on the eve of departure, and eventually, I resorted to the occasional Xanax to get through a long flight.

Again, this is where having a good partner, one who shares your vision and your work ethic, is so crucial. When I just couldn't be there, Harris could step right in. He knew the brand as well as I did and was equally committed to OPI's success. He was able to step in and take over if I was ill or unable to travel. And when we did travel together, he was always willing to put up with my grueling schedule in order to get back home quickly.

He even put up with my bizarre eating schedule. When I was on these trips I operated on pure adrenaline and never felt hungry until the end of the day, when the work was done and I could finally turn off. Harris, meanwhile, needed three squares a day—he got light-headed and cranky otherwise.

One morning we got up at the crack of dawn to take a redeye from Toronto to New York, where we were scheduled to do a huge presentation. Harris woke with a really nasty eye infection, and by the time we landed he looked like he'd been in a back-alley fight, with his eyes nearly swollen shut and oozing.

"Don't worry about the presentation," I said. "I'll do it, you rest."

He nodded miserably, and when we got to the hotel I asked Harris if there was anything I could do.

"Just get me a bagel," he said in a weak voice.

"Absolutely," I said. "Anything you need."

But in my haste to get ready and get to the meeting on time, I completely forgot the bagel. When I returned and started updating Harris on how the meeting had gone, poor Harris, who was still in bed, interrupted me. "Well that's all well and good, Suzi, but where's my bagel?"

"They ran out," I said.

His mouth dropped open. "You're telling me all of New York City ran out of bagels."

"Completely out," I said.

He still hasn't forgiven me for that one.

None of our "road warrior" travel ever prevented Harris from being finicky about his accommodations, either. For the Greek Isles collection, we were on planes for who knows how many hours and arrived in Athens during the wee hours. I was ready to drop where I stood, but true to form, Harris had to inspect our rooms top to bottom. I can't even recall what the matter was now, but no room was up to his standards. An exasperated bellhop followed us from rejected room to rejected room, and finally asked, "Sir, do you think you'll find a room tonight?"

Harris whirled upon him. "We're not sure," he said, and went back to scrutinizing the linens.

This Is Not Whine Country

All during my kids' growing-up years, OPI was growing, too. More collections, more countries, more promotion, more lacquers . . . and our customers paid us the profound compliment of only wanting more. Eventually I'd be doing seven collections a year, in addition to periodic mini-collections that were designed for a certain theme or product tie-in. Every year seemed busier than the last, and when Andrea and Andrew became old enough to be involved in what felt like *thousands* of extracurricular activities, I feared I'd met my match. I was faced with dilemmas constantly: Do I miss my kid's baseball game or do I miss the PR meeting? Do I go to the recital or do I meet with the Paris distributor? Should I keep pushing and test this color one more time, or do I go home and get some sleep?

Though I often had to choose between my family and the business, or between the business and things I would have done for myself, I still can't really complain. I loved the work and I loved to go to work every day, and I felt a deep responsibility to OPI and its employees to do my job well. I felt so lucky to be able to pour my energies into something I was passionate about.

That said, when you work and travel as much as I did and still want to prioritize family, sacrifices are simply inevitable. Anything that could be categorized under "me" time was always the first to go. I never went to the gym, didn't have a facial in more than twenty years, ate on the fly and skipped plenty of meals, and *always* skimped on sleep. (Like I said, I wouldn't recommend this life for everyone!)

These were sacrifices I was more than willing to make, but one thing I know I missed out on was friendships with other women. I was and continue to be very close with my sister, Miriam, but as far as meeting girlfriends for dinner or going away on a girls' weekend trip, it just didn't happen. I had so little time for socializing and felt like I couldn't relate to most women I knew anyway. Thankfully things are now different, but back then it was quite unusual for a woman to be at the helm of a large company, so I remember often feeling like an outsider.

People ask me if I'd do anything differently. My answer is no. DID I DO EVERYTHING RIGHT? No. Did I do most things right? Yes, and I did it all with 100 percent passion, and that is more than enough.

And how could I not? I worked seven days a week, sometimes from early morning until 10 or 11 at night, and even when I wasn't at the office I only wanted to talk about work. Once, in an attempt to make time for friends, I organized a girlfriends' group that would meet once a month. I never made it to a single meeting. The group was a great success, however, and everyone thanked me for organizing it.

I realized that if I was to have any friends, they'd have to be work friends. And that's just what happened: outside of my family, my closest friend on earth is none other than Harris Shepard. We've been best friends for nearly thirty years now, and I really couldn't ask for a better one. We are like brother and sister, without the sibling rivalry. In Harris I found one of the world's kindest human beings. He is as smart as he is practical and one of the best public relations agents in the business. We grew up together, and we both had our lives transformed by OPI.

Far more worrisome to me was missing out on some of the kids' activities and events. There were piano recitals and sports tournaments I couldn't attend, but I'm certain this bothered me more than it bothered them. The fact is, my kids grew up with a working mother—they never knew anything different. Any time I was away, I had the comfort of knowing they were always surrounded by a warm, loving family, and I made an effort to speak to them daily. No matter how busy I was, I'd always take a call from any family member. It's a practice I continue to this day, and my entire extended family is in the habit of telling each other how much we love each other. So I'm confident my children always knew they were loved and that though I had to be away at times, they were my first priority.

And to be quite frank, I just wasn't the kind of mother who was cut out to volunteer weekly at my kids' schools or join the PTA or assist in the classroom anyway. Believe me, I know my weaknesses—no one wants me cooking or doing accounting or trying to be a parent volunteer. The one time I did volunteer was a complete disaster. Andrea, a fourth-grader at the time, pointed out that all the other moms volunteered, and couldn't I, just *once*? Well, how could I say no? So I cleared my schedule and dutifully showed up at the school office. The administrative assistant asked me to make copies and then left me in a closet with an industrial-sized Xerox machine. I didn't have the slightest clue how to operate the thing, but I figured I'd give it the old college try. Forty seconds later there were papers flying everywhere—literally shooting out of the machine! It had taken me less than a minute to make a terrible mess, and I felt horrible about wasting paper.

I was too embarrassed to admit how I'd bungled this simple job, which left me with the dilemma of what to do. There was one solution: I stuffed all the ruined papers into my jacket, snuck out of the school, and hightailed it to the OPI campus. There I begged the indefatigable Ilene Richkind, whom I called "Little Stuff" because she was only five feet tall but a total workplace powerhouse, to make fifty copies pronto. She did, laughing the whole time, and even took care of the incriminating evidence. (By which I mean she smoothed out the wrinkled papers and used them for scratch paper. We didn't waste anything.) Then I flew back to the school, where I presented the administrative assistant with fifty fresh copies, still warm from the OPI Xerox machine. It took me an hour, but I finished the job, and then told Andrea and the teacher I was sorry but wouldn't be volunteering again.

In the end, I was quite okay with not being Parent Volunteer of the Year. I was far more useful—to my family at home as well as my family at OPI—at the office. The fact is, everything I did, I did for the greater good of my two families. I keenly felt the responsibility of caring for our employees, who were unflaggingly loyal and who gave us 100 percent. I was happy to give them 110 percent in return and do whatever it took to ensure success for the collective. Similarly, my family at home knew I was doing all of this work for them. The success of OPI gave my children opportunities I could never have dreamed of

We want our children to FOLLOW their dreams, PURSUE their passions, GIVE BACK to others, and LIVE a life of personal and professional fulfillment. One of the best ways to set them up for this kind of success is to model it for them.

as a child, and it made life easier for my parents, who had worked so hard and had been through so much. Knowing that I was doing all of this for them made tough choices such as missing the game or the recital a little easier. And as Andrea and Andrew grew older, they came to understand the enormity of my role at OPI, and they respected me for what I was accomplishing.

Ultimately, that allowed me to let go of the guilt, because despite all the juggling that my job required, I know that OPI made me a better person, and it made me a better mother. I grew into my true self, the person I was meant to be, through the work I did at OPI. Children learn from the example of seeing their parents pursue their dreams and follow their life's passions, and they flourish with parents who are authentic, contented, and happy. A life of personal and professional fulfillment, of passion and creativity, and of using your resources to give back—this is the kind of life we want for our children, is it not? I was proud to model that for my kids and to raise them to be good people.

On a much more practical level, I learned to choose my battles. When Andrea was scheduled to compete in a regional tennis tournament that conflicted with a major OPI meeting, for example, there was no way I was going to miss the tournament . . . but I still wanted to get back to OPI as soon as possible. So, as I dropped her off at the courts I said, "Okay, go beat the shit out of that girl, and then *let's go!*"

She did, and we did, and then I got back to work.

Girl Without Limits

Now that I've helped lead OPI for more than thirty years *and* raised two children who are flourishing, I'm often asked about my thoughts on "women in business." To be quite honest, I never thought of myself as "a woman in business." Not once. I simply saw myself as a businessperson, a worker. Did I realize I was an anomaly at the time as a female business leader, even in the realms of fashion and beauty? Of course I did. But my focus was never on my gender or on any potential limitations my gender imposed on my ability to own and operate a company. I didn't think there were any. Above and beyond anything else, I focused on the *work*. My job was to complete the task at hand— and then the next and the next

> *Women in business today have a tremendous capacity to launch, build, and lead businesses and to be POWERFUL AGENTS OF CHANGE.*

and the next—and overall, to build the brand of OPI and to bring our customers colors that helped them express themselves and feel empowered.

When George Schaeffer and I first got to know the distributors in the salon industry, it's true that most of them were men. These were family businesses that were handed down from father to son. It felt like an old boys' club because it was. As such I never joined "the boys" in their after-hours beer drinking and bar-hopping. I saw nothing but an advantage to that. I showed up to every meeting sharper and more clear-headed than they were, able to negotiate until I got exactly what I wanted.

Did I encounter sexism in the industry? Of course I did, especially in those early days. During my very first presentation to sales reps—I was still in my twenties, still new to the business, and very nervous—a man interrupted me and asked, in front of the entire meeting, when was the last time I'd gotten laid. "Truthfully," I shot back, "it's been a while," and immediately returned to my presentation.

If this happened to me today my reaction would be quite different—probably unprintable. But at the time I answered off the cuff, my audience laughed, and I got positive feedback afterward for not getting rattled. None of this mattered to me. What mattered was the work, and I did what I always did, which was focus on the work. I in fact took this man's offensive remark as a sign that my presentation was so boring he felt the need to liven things up (however crudely). I resolved to make my sales presentations more engaging. I still have this attitude. If someone ever put me down, it made me work all the harder.

Thankfully episodes like this one were few and far between, and certainly so among OPI employees. The culture we created at OPI was so familial that people did not disrespect one another. Further, our entire mission was to empower women through color and self-expression. We were a business focused on women, and it would have been foolish and self-defeating for our people to think less of women or treat them as lesser than their own customers. If you are selling to women, you cannot disrespect them.

It was also abundantly clear to anyone connected with the business that George and I had a zero-tolerance policy on sexual harassment. I can recall but a single incident that occurred back in the '90s, when one of the factory supervisors was accused of sexual harassment. He was immediately removed from his post and investigated, and quickly thereafter fired.

I'm very happy to say that OPI was a company that was always dedicated to women's empowerment. I've discussed how we supported our customers' empowerment, but here I'm referring to our employees. One of the big changes we made was to put women in management positions from the beginning. It made sense: women are typically the ones who are managing households, from financial decisions to scheduling to people, and they're intimately involved in making decisions. Moreover, as the vast majority of our customer base was female, women were the best people to connect to other women. When you're selling something, you've got to believe in it and be passionate about it. Women understood nail polish more readily than men because it was a product with which they were already familiar. Male or female, I made the sales force try out the lacquers. Especially in the early days the sales force was mostly men, and they laughed at first about having colored nails. But they stopped laughing once they saw the results of our product compared to other brands. Suddenly they saw how much better it was—the ease of use, the intensity of the color, the quality of any special effect, the overall wow effect. All at once they understood the product better and could, therefore, sell it better.

One of our most amazing employees was a woman named Linda Lennox, and her first job was to run traffic and manage the routes for inbound and outbound freight. She was so good at it and commanded so much respect that when she walked into the conference room to negotiate fees for the coming year, all the truckers leapt to their feet and wouldn't sit until Linda did. But really, there was very little "negotiation." Linda said these are the fees I want, and she got them. She was so smart and so savvy that she went on to become a vice president of traffic and inventory control.

Today, I think we are at an amazing point in time for female business leaders. Do we still have work to do? Absolutely. But today, women have more opportunities than ever before to launch, build, and lead businesses. We possess inherent skills and natural abilities that the business world values. We are great networkers. We have a higher ability to multitask. We're good at delegating, budgeting, negotiating, and managing—after all, so many of us manage families, which are a world of complexity if there ever were one. And, we are great leaders. Women are more likely to choose a positive leadership style and less likely to succumb to untested assumptions. Today's businesswoman is strong and confident and has the ability to make decisions using the same intellect, education, and resources that men have. We have the tremendous capacity to be powerful agents of change as more and more of us take on leadership positions. There are no limits for women today.

As the years went on and the reputation of OPI grew, people started to become more interested in me personally. Who was the Suzi behind Suzi the First Lady of Nails? I admit that at first I didn't get it. In my own mind (and certainly in the mind of my family) I was just Suzi Weiss-Fischmann. In fact I *still* feel this way—what's the big deal?—but in 2006 I had an experience at a women's business roundtable that opened my eyes to something that, frankly, I'd simply been too busy, too immersed in the thick of things at the office, to see.

There were maybe two hundred women in attendance, all leaders in their fields, and I delivered the keynote address over a luncheon meeting. I shared my usual story of OPI's unusual beginnings, and I spoke a little about where I came from and how every day I was amazed and grateful to have ended up where I was. I noticed that this audience seemed to be unusually attentive. Then during the Q&A, I received question after question on how I'd "broken into" a male-dominated industry, how I handled any sexism in the workplace, and how I dealt with the pressures of being a "female business icon" while remaining deeply involved in family life. I nearly turned around to see whom they were referring to—was there a female business icon standing behind me at the podium?

I swallowed my incredulity and answered every question the best way I knew how—honestly and authentically—and was then blown away to receive a standing ovation. Many audience members wanted to speak with me afterward, and almost to a woman they thanked me for being a pioneer for female business leaders and an inspiration for them and their daughters. It was the mention of daughters that really got to me. Though I had been far too busy to stop and think about the impression I was conveying to the world—and due to my upbringing, hadn't given much thought to being "a woman in business"—it was clear that these issues were very much on the forefront of public consciousness. The response to that keynote address enabled me to see the bigger picture, and it brought home to me the importance of being a role model and an inspiration to young women. I had always been interested in empowering women through the products I created at OPI—now I saw how the very act of creating empowered women and girls by setting an example of what women could achieve. After that, I never underestimated my role as an inspiration to the next generations of business leaders, especially young girls.

My advice for women getting started in business, especially if this is your first job or you're making a major career shift, is to stay focused on your vision for the future. Your vision will set the course for the rest of your life, affecting everything from your career to your long-term relationships to having a family of your own.

And if you're not proficient at it yet, learn patience. Someone once said, "Patience is a virtue that successful people cannot be without." It's all the more relevant today, as we live in a world of instant gratification. If our browser loads a page in four seconds rather than 0.367, we become irritated. Dropped calls are a new source of frustration. But though the Internet and social media can be time-savers and have increased

PATIENCE is not only a virtue, it's a business skill. When launching a business, you must have patience to build relationships, become profitable, overcome the inevitable bumps in the road, and stay committed to a long-term vision rather than chase a short-term goal.

the speed of transactions and processes, we still need to take the time to communicate with people and build long-term partnerships. OPI was built on relationships, which required an investment of time and a commitment to a long-term vision rather than short-term gains. The same was true for PR back then—sometimes it would be six months before we'd begin to see momentum building, but once it did, it caught fire! Patience is required to see results.

We must also have patience when it comes to making money and to overcoming the inevitable bumps in the road associated with a new business. Yes, it's *possible* for a good idea to go viral and succeed quickly, but this is the exception, not the rule. So, when you're just starting out, secure a year's worth (or better yet, two) of seed money—not three or six months' worth. If you don't have money, bye-bye, you're done.

Also, don't expect to make money right away. For the vast majority of new businesses, growth is a matter of many, many baby steps before you're able to make those huge leaps forward. So many businesses today operate on short-term quarterly earnings goals rather than envisioning a grand idea and consistently going for it. That was never our way. It was years before OPI was profitable, and many years before it became a global smash. Setbacks along the journey are just part of the deal, and you must have the patience, the commitment to a long-term goal—and the capital—to weather those temporary losses.

If you're convinced that your ideas and your products are good, as George Schaeffer and I were, don't give up. There is so much reward to be found in working your way through adversity, in persisting no matter what. Eleanor Roosevelt is credited with saying, "A woman is like a tea bag. You never know how strong she is until she gets in hot water." I thought of that quote many times over the years. How true it is! Every time I faced a challenge, I didn't back down—and I always emerged stronger. And any time I started to get a little discouraged, I'd hold the example of my parents before me. I drew great inspiration from their ability to live through unimaginable tragedy and still emerge as positive, loving people.

Finally, do have a partner. Launching and running a business is very hard work. It can eat up all of your time and your energy. But it's so much easier if there are two (or more) of you. You can divide and conquer, share the burden, and assign tasks according to your unique strengths. It takes a team to manage a family or to run a business, and certainly to do both concurrently, and I never once believed I could do everything on my own. With family life and at work, I surrounded myself with people who could help me. There is nothing you cannot accomplish if you have the passion and drive for it, you put in the hard work, and you surround yourself with the right team. Nothing whatsoever.

— six —

DON'T BOSSA NOVA
ME AROUND

A S WE HEADED TOWARD THE NEW MILLENNIUM, GEORGE and I still shared an office and our desks remained side by side. But by then we'd graduated to a larger space that allowed us both to stand in the room *and* open the door fully—a true benchmark of success.

By this time OPI had grown to take up several city blocks, and the OPI family—our employees—numbered in the hundreds. The business had grown so quickly, and we certainly couldn't have kept up with it without our employees, who were the most loyal and hardworking in the beauty industry. At our height, we'd be seven hundred employees strong, operating on a campus sprawling across seven acres. We had to convince the city to install a traffic light on Saticoy Street to manage all the vehicles going into and out of the facilities.

No matter how big we grew, George and I ran OPI like the family business it was. In fact, if I had to describe our company culture and our leadership styles, I'd say all seven hundred of us were one big crazy family, with George and me the Papa Bear and Mama Bear loosely presiding over a madcap family reunion. We all worked hard, but the atmosphere was warm, fun, and often hilarious. On any given day, you'd find George, in his trademark crazy suspenders and painted nails, laughing at the top of his lungs as he headed out the door to catch a plane. Or me, pacing the halls, muttering to myself as I thought my way through another collection. Coming through the door were the sales reps, the foot soldiers of our operation, returning with real-time news and reviews from the salon owners. Turn a corner and you'd see the R&D team in their crisp white lab coats, testing out a new finish. In a conference room you'd find brand managers hammering out a new concept—and the second they got it, the fastest guy was off to alert a member of the marketing team. Head to the breakroom and there were the factory workers, coming in for coffee and some of the homemade brownies a receptionist brought in. It was a circus every day, full of good food and hilarity and high energy. Neither George nor I wanted to work at a job that felt like drudgery, or at a business that operated like a corporate machine. We wanted to look forward to going to work and to engage in work that was both meaningful and fun. We knew our employees wanted the same things.

So we quite deliberately fostered an environment of collegiality, respect, and equality, all within a warm family atmosphere. At OPI there was no such thing as an executive team and "everyone else." George and I believed in the fundamental equality and inherent worth of all workers, and we treated them all as equals. We all had our roles to play, and each job was just as important as any other. So, even at our largest we remained a flat organization, with no hierarchies and layers of bureaucracy to navigate. This allowed us to make things happen quickly if we needed to, and it sent a clear signal that every employee was equally valuable.

We also maintained an open-door policy. Any OPI employee was welcome to drop in any time, for whatever reason. Suggestion, idea, complaint, request, or if they just wanted to chat, they could (and did) bring it all. If an employee had a better idea than we did, we implemented it immediately and gave credit where credit was due. All of this worked because we hired good people who were as dedicated to OPI's vision as we were. OPI was never a place where you'd drop whatever you were doing at 5 p.m. and make a break for the door. Everyone finished the task at hand, tidied up their workspace, and left to begin again the next morning. If someone needed to come in on Saturday to finish, they did so voluntarily.

I really came to love the OPI family as my own. Over the years, we went through it all together—births, deaths, marriages, buying homes, graduations, divorces, sending kids to college, sickness, recovery, and eventually, retirement. We loved to promote from within, and many people made OPI their lifelong careers. The genuine love between us, and the dreams we made come true for so many, is what I am most proud of when I look back over a thirty-seven-year career.

As OPI became more successful, we rewarded our employees commensurately, adding more benefits as we were able. At the end of the day your organization is only as good as its people, and we did whatever we could to invest in our employees. We really believed in them, and there was such mutual respect among all of us. We introduced profit-sharing and provided employees with 401k plans. We offered no-interest, long-term loans for employees buying their first home or car. We set up scholarships for employees' children and gave them computers and printers if they maintained at least a B average. True to our lifelong obsession with food, we built a cafeteria that offered subsidized meals. In addition to good food, the cafeteria provided an informal meeting place where people could relax and chat and come together. The cafeteria is still operating, and it's where I grab lunch when I'm at the office.

We were also keenly aware that many of our employees were immigrants who'd come to America for a better life just as we had, and many were sending money back home to support relatives. Because George and I were so accessible, every employee knew they could ask us for anything and we would help. It wasn't at all uncommon, for example, for employees to come to us if something went amiss back home—such as a sick family member who needed treatment, or a child who needed money for school. The spirit of *tzedakah*, or charitable giving, imbued everything we did, and we always said yes. And really, how could we not? We were immigrants ourselves, as well as the children of immigrants who came to this country with nothing after enduring terrible tragedies. We will be forever grateful for the opportunities America made possible.

So, in that spirit, any employee who got their US citizenship received a $500 savings bond in celebration. Every July 4th, every employee in the company, no matter if they took out the garbage or were a member of the executive team, received a $250 bonus. In addition to celebrating this great country that was making life possible for all of us, this was a way to demonstrate that all employees were equal, and that we could not do this without every single person performing his or her role. End-of-year bonuses were determined by merit, but everyone received something.

Of course things didn't always go perfectly. Mistakes happened, but our attitude was they weren't a big deal as long as you told someone right away and worked to fix the situation. And of course, everything is an experience and we learn from mistakes. Some, however, weren't fixable, and were a source of deep disappointment. We once fired the entire night crew after discovering that someone had been stealing, for example. It didn't matter that the thief could have been just one person—the others had known about it and had kept their silence, allowing it to happen. So they all went.

Thankfully those sorts of instances were quite rare. Overall we really were a big, happy family, one that happened to board a rocket ship at the same time. Our people were the biggest part of the OPI success story. We laughed every single day. We had fun. Together we created something unique in the beauty industry. We made people, including ourselves, happy. And *that* is what translated into every bottle of lacquer we ever produced and made OPI the global success it continues to be.

Pale to the Chief

While all this expansion was occurring, I was coming into my own as both a business and a civic leader. Like everything else it was happening in the midst of the chaos, and I was learning on the fly. But I do think there were core aspects of my leadership style that came naturally and grew to maturity within the family environment at OPI.

For one, I never, ever micromanaged. I really believe in hiring the very best people and then letting them do their thing. By "the very best," I mean people who can do the job better than anyone and who fit into your company culture by sharing your vision and your enthusiasm to carry it out. The only thing I need to see is the results. Giving employees their autonomy gives them your vote of confidence and empowers them to take ownership of their responsibilities and become personally invested in their jobs. Empowering employees is one of the best things a manager can do, and personally, I find it such a turnoff when managers get too involved in employees' day-to-day jobs or nitpick every detail. Far better is to hire employees you can trust and then let them grow and mature in their positions.

I also led by example. With the exception of computers and accounting—which for the good of everyone I left entirely to others—I could do any task I expected of employees. Over the years I'd done everything, from the physical labor of sweeping the floors and filling and labeling bottles, to the mental work of researching color trends and devising marketing strategies, to the plain old footwork of traveling the world to promote and sell our products. My feeling is that you can't very well train someone in a task, and certainly can't critique them or show them a better way, unless you know experientially what you're doing.

And as the boss, you are the model. This is a job that never ends. You are always on display; employees look to you as the standard-bearer and as the one who inspires. Whether it's your enthusiasm for the job, your role in communicating the brand's vision, or your personal work ethic, employees are looking to you as their role model. When you stride through those doors the spotlight is on you, and you need to be on your A-game. Especially in the early years, I had quite a few doubts. There were plenty of nights I didn't sleep a wink and stayed awake fretting. But in the morning I put all of that aside—it was showtime. I went to work with a positive attitude, ready to make it happen no matter what and to be the best role model I could be for the team.

My own role model when it came to a strong work ethic was my father. More than anyone, he instilled in me the ability to work hard. "Things don't just happen," he said. "You have to make them happen." This lesson became all the more poignant for me after his death in 2003. He had worked as a butcher his entire life, as had his father before him. He loved the work and he was very, very good at it. He could take one look at a cow and tell its age or how much milk it could give. To reach that level of skill, you must put in many hours. When I got tired at OPI or overwhelmed, I thought of him, and then I thought of all the employees who were looking up to me as an example, and I kept going. My dad is still missed every day, but his spirit lives on in OPI.

I also led based on a desire for success for the greater good, and thus I was always willing to listen to any idea, even if it directly contradicted one of my own. I used to tell everyone that one of the worst things you can do is to yes me. I actually love being challenged. Make me stop and think, disagree with me, tell me I'm full of it—this is how the best ideas happen. If the idea resulted in a better outcome for employees or in advancing OPI's vision,

My business superpower is making decisions. I move quickly and don't waste any time overthinking. Are mistakes possible? Of course! But I'D MUCH RATHER ACT NOW and risk a potential mistake THAN NOT ACT AT ALL and miss an opportunity.

consider it done. Any goal achieved was a success for the entire OPI family.

But if I have any business superpower, I'd have to say it's *making decisions*. People often ask me to identify my greatest success, and this is my answer, every time. I never waste time overthinking options—I make decisions quickly and with confidence. I was once addressing the global marketing team of a company that's home to nearly two dozen billion-dollar brands. The room was full of brilliant, savvy people with hugely successful careers. During the Q&A they all wanted to know my best business advice, and I only had two things to offer: "Stay entrepreneurial in your divisions and make fucking decisions." The room erupted in spontaneous applause.

Any time I was presented with a list of options, whether it was two or ten, I immediately made a choice and we moved on it. I always had such a sense of urgency, and my attitude was that if you didn't make a decision you could miss an opportunity. I told my employees and my children that you don't necessarily have to do it right, but you do have to make a decision—that's how you get ahead. Are mistakes possible? Of course! But I was never afraid of the consequences, because nobody is perfect and you learn from your mistakes.

For our Texas collection of 2011, for example, I tried a different texture for some of the lacquers. I'm all for innovation, but my mistake was in not alerting the consumer to expect something different. Very quickly we heard back from distributors, salon owners, and individual consumers. When they saw a texture they weren't used to, everyone assumed something had gone wrong with the formula. Telling people *after the fact* that the new texture was intentional was far too little too late: once you have to explain something you've lost the opportunity and you've lost the confidence of the consumer. As you'd guess, the sales on those lacquers were not good, and we discontinued them. In retrospect, I should have alerted the consumer to expect something different, which would have given her the choice on whether or not to risk her dollars on something new. As it was, I did not give her that choice and she was unhappy, because in essence she'd paid for something else.

When mistakes did happen, we learned from them and made a change but did not dwell on them, which can be just as dangerous. Instead we very quickly regrouped and moved on. My father had a saying: "That train has gone, so catch the next one." There is always another chance.

For the most part, though, I made good decisions, and I trusted my intuition. Some of my decisions even went against the advice of everyone around me—but especially when it came to color, I always trusted my instincts. One of the best examples concerns a lacquer from our 2008 French collection that became one of the most iconic and game-changing colors in nail care. I was absolutely obsessed with this rich gray-brown and made thirteen different variations in an attempt to get it exactly right. Not a single person at OPI liked any of them—everyone said that I'd made "poop in a bottle." But our fans went wild for the color we dubbed You Don't Know Jacques!, which started the ongoing greige trend. This lacquer has already been deemed a classic in the beauty industry, and it's a bestseller every year.

What if I had listened to the naysayers and missed that opportunity? There *could* have been another chance, but by then, perhaps the moment would be gone, or more likely, a competitor would've gotten there before OPI did. Bottom line, it's far better to act decisively and risk making a mistake than not act at all.

Suzi—The First Lady of Nails

Back in the early '90s when we were still a young company, I found myself wondering how I would ever make my voice heard at those enormous trade shows and huge distributor meetings. Or anywhere, for that matter! I believed wholeheartedly in the quality of our products, to the point I was convinced they were better than anything on the market. The problem was, I was still reserved and shy—and fearful of public speaking. I think the last time I'd spoken in front of a group, it was in a high school public speaking class. I remember feeling shaky and nauseated. I got through the class, but let's just say it was not an A for me.

Still I yearned for the chance to speak. I wanted salon owners and nail techs to know who I was, and more urgently, I wanted them to know the name OPI. When one day I was sharing these concerns with Harris, he immediately waved them away. "All of that's just noise, Suzi," he said. "All you need to do is focus on your true self. Then the words will flow."

Harris was a big believer in *true self*. He is the one who first taught me that focusing on your true self—and bringing that person to bear on all aspects of the business, even its ancillary tasks like public speaking—would result not just in greater personal happiness but in greater business success. Be your authentic self, he always said.

And really, there is no other person you can be. You can try to inhabit a persona for a while, but the truth always emerges. So Harris was right. My job was to be faithful to my true self and to the vision I had for OPI, and to focus on those things, rather than on my quaking knees, when I had to stand before audiences. I took comfort in the words of former prime minister Golda Meir: "Trust yourself. Create the kind of self that you will be happy to live with all your life. Make the most of yourself by fanning the tiny, inner sparks of possibility into flames of achievement."

Always BE YOUR AUTHENTIC SELF. There is no one else you can be, and the world needs your unique skills and contributions.

I knew I was a strong and very disciplined person, and I knew I could draw on those "inner sparks of possibility" to get over my fear. I was very determined not to let it get the better of me, and I resolved not to back down. Ironically enough, one thing that helped enormously was the spotlight. The next time I was on a stage, the lights were so bright I couldn't see the audience anyway! So I pretended no one was out there, and I was just going to say my thing. That speech went well, and each time I had to speak, it got better. The knees didn't shake as much, and the words came out more clearly and with more confidence. As they say, practice makes perfect.

I also think *the story itself* helped me get over my fear. I noticed that any time I was telling OPI's story—our unique beginnings, the DNA of our brand—the words came easily. Which brings me back to Harris's very fine point about being your true self. When I was telling the story of how OPI came to be and how I—Suzi Weiss-Fischmann, and no one else—had created all those colors that changed the industry, I was telling my own story. Not someone else's. I was authentic and enthusiastic, and the story always made a connection with people. As you'll see, I ended up landing some of OPI's best deals simply by telling my story.

The positive feedback I received also went a long way in helping me overcome my fear of public speaking. At business meetings people would thank me afterward for my clear and engaging presentations. At civic and educational gatherings, people would tell me how inspiring they'd found my story. So I channeled all that positive feedback and drew upon it, working to make every speech

> *As I grew into my TRUE SELF, the LEADER and the person I was meant to be, OPI became more successful. That's no coincidence.*

better than the last. And now, I actually enjoy public speaking and look forward to it! It's yet another development on this crazy, adventurous journey with OPI that I never would've been able to predict.

I really believe that my true self, the person I was meant to be, came into being and grew into maturity as OPI did. My voice, my presence in the industry, my business sense, my sense of style, my understanding of all the multiple roles I was to play . . . it all evolved together. And every year, as I felt that I was growing into and expressing more of my true self, OPI became more and more successful. I don't believe that's a coincidence.

In the late '90s, as Harris and I were leaving a lunch meeting in Manhattan, a magazine editor quipped, "Suzi, you know you're the first lady of nails!" I laughed it off, but Harris looked at me and replied, with great seriousness, "You really are. You know that, right?" I thought of how shy I'd been just a few years before, how I wondered if anyone in the nail care industry would ever remember my name. I had to stop and marvel at all the things that had happened.

Somewhere along the way other people referred to me as the first lady of nails, and once it found its way into print, the name stuck. Now people throughout the world know me as Suzi the First Lady of Nails. When I was little Zsuzsi, never could I have dreamed of such a thing, nor that I'd have such an influence on an entire industry. But I suppose we all have a destiny, and the First Lady of Nails is mine.

My Chihuahua Bites!

Harris would be the first to tell you that I'm a very kind person—99 percent of the time. But for that 1 percent, watch out! I've heard him tell people I'm "a killer" who can "haul any CEO's ass to the curb." It's true that I suffer no fools—and I can be ruthless if I need to be. I am not intimidated by anyone, no matter how successful or famous or powerful.

The truth is, when you're at the helm of a multi million-dollar operation and you have employees and vendors and consumers counting on you, there will be times when you must be aggressive. Or, if you prefer, *supremely motivated*. I'm acutely aware that women leaders can get a bad rap for having basic business expectations such as insisting on superior results, asking that a job be completed on time or ASAP, or earning equal pay. For this we've been labeled aggressive, demanding, pushy, and much worse. Ridiculous! I never let any of this slow me down for a millisecond. I was 100 percent focused on completing the task at hand, and then the next one and the next one. I had no time to worry about labels and people's perceptions of me, or anything else for that matter. The reputation I worked to cultivate was someone who would get the job done—every time, no matter what.

Once, George and I, along with an OPI salesperson, our VP of sales and marketing, and an account manager, were in a meeting with a beauty brand that's worth billions of dollars. (For obvious reasons I'll remain vague on some of the details, but trust me, you've shopped there.) Our two companies were considering a partnership, and it would be a huge deal for both of us. George and I were eager to collaborate. But the problem was, the company wanted to co-opt a marketing strategy that had been a recognizable part of OPI's advertising campaigns for many years. What's more, this strategy didn't even make sense for their company. They had hundreds of physical locations in the United States and a lot of walk-in traffic. Their job was to keep those people in the stores and get them to buy something. As our products were sold mainly by distributors to salons, we were doing an entirely different thing. I kept telling the CEO that not only was our marketing strategy not available for his use, it simply wouldn't work for them—it was a classic case of apples and oranges. He wouldn't back down, but neither would I. We got into a huge argument, and once he realized he was getting nowhere with me, he and his team walked out of the meeting.

In his haste, he left behind the piece of paper on which he'd been taking notes and doodling. On it he'd written, in blocky capitals, BITCH, BITCH, WHAT A BITCH. I showed this to George and the rest of the team and we all laughed. I considered it nothing but a compliment. I had stood my ground and didn't give in to the CEO's unreasonable—and unwise—demands. I was not willing to give another company the free use of our intellectual property, no matter how much it would impact the bottom line.

The OPI team was with me. I didn't even have to pause to consult them to know this was true. This demonstrates the importance of company culture. George and I surrounded ourselves with people who would carry out our vision. I knew they had my back. So we walked out of that conference room with no deal, and with no regrets.

And guess what happened? About a year later, the company came back to us. This time they were willing to listen and to work together to come up with an entirely new marketing strategy, one that made sense for both of us.

The CEO never apologized, but I had never expected an apology—nor did I need one. What I needed to see was the results. I stood my ground, and we ended up having a long, lucrative run with the brand, one that was a win for everyone.

seven

MY ADDRESS
IS "HOLLYWOOD"

M Y OFFICE—OR MORE CORRECTLY, MY CORNER OF THE
office George and I shared—somehow became a cen-
tral hub for hatching new ideas. Various people would
drop by for impromptu brainstorming meetings, and this
is how some of our best marketing ideas came to be. I
was constantly thinking about new ways we could reach
the consumer, and I always encouraged everyone to think
of unconventional ways to bring attention to the brand.
"Let's think *smart*," I always told the team. "Let's think
different."

One day, a few of us were sitting around my desk bouncing around ideas. How could we be a part of our consumer's life not just when she was at the salon but when she was doing other things she enjoyed—shopping for clothes, listening to her favorite singer, seeing her favorite movie. And suddenly we all lit up. The movies! We were located right there in Hollywood—it made perfect sense to partner with a local studio. And with the movie industry's focus on glamour, red-carpet fashion, and fantasy, we made a perfect match.

Our task then was to start making inquiries, not only to form relationships with producers and studio executives but to find a script that would be the perfect complement to OPI's vision. We began the old-fashioned way, by making phone calls. Email was around by then, but we wanted person-to-person contact: the warmth and enthusiasm of a person on the other end of the line, a memorable conversation that wouldn't get lost in the shuffle of an inbox. So Harris began cold-calling the marketing departments of every major studio in Hollywood. Because OPI was already a known brand with a lot of buzz—and because Harris is very good at his job—he always got through.

And that is how we learned about a movie that seemed to be made for the job. Titled *Legally Blonde*, the film starred Reese Witherspoon, who was already a favorite at OPI because of her performance as Tracy Flick in *Election*. Although filming was already complete, when we heard about Elle Woods—an intelligent, ambitious, fashion-conscious young woman—we knew we'd be a great match. The movie's core audience was also our target market. Many of its viewers would be young women who were in college or just starting out in their careers. Maybe this girl couldn't yet afford the designer bag or blouse, and maybe she couldn't yet afford dinner at Il Cielo, but she could afford a salon manicure and a night at the movies. OPI could be her entry into the world of high fashion and professional beauty products, her first way to accessorize using a designer product. And quite auspiciously, one of the movie's most beloved characters—the unforgettable Paulette Bonafonté—was Elle's manicurist, confidante, and partner in crime. It was almost too good to be true.

Harris had barely hung up the phone when I started pestering him: Did we have a meeting yet? When was our meeting? Had they agreed to a meeting yet? I must have called him twenty times over the space of two days. But we got that meeting, and I could barely contain my excitement as I described to the studio execs our vision of a mutually beneficial partnership. It also didn't hurt that Harris and I came bearing lots of free samples.

Long story short, the producers agreed to a partnership. It was too late to shoot new scenes or launch a collection for this film, but it just so happened that OPI was already in the movie. Near the beginning when Elle is painting her nails, there are three OPI shades prominently featured. And later, in the famous "bend and snap" scene at Paulette's salon, OPI lacquers can be seen on display.

There was plenty of time, however, for an exclusive *Legally Blonde 2* collection and full advertising campaign, and that happened in 2003. The colors and the names were based on the palette and the humor of the movie:

Blonde Date, Red-Y for Anything, and Elle's Pearls. This was the first time a professional nail company partnered with a major Hollywood studio—and we started a trend that's still ongoing.

Our next big movie collaboration was with Disney for *Alice in Wonderland*. Of all the talented people involved in the movies we went on to do—and the list would include *Pirates of the Caribbean*, *The Muppets*, *OZ: The Great and Powerful*, *Shrek Forever After*, *Burlesque*, *The Amazing Spider-Man*, and the *Skyfall 007* Bond franchise—director Tim Burton was the most involved, and the most detail-oriented. I absolutely loved that. He was very particular about the proportions in the advertising—the nail polish bottle, the tea cup, Alice herself. At OPI we were all just as detail-oriented as he was, and we worked well together.

That collaboration also resulted in one of my proudest professional moments. Disney studios require an audit when they collaborate with another company. It was a weeklong process, and it included extended visits to the OPI factory and interviews with employees. The auditors were amazed to be corrected by our employees time and time again: "We don't work for OPI," they said. "We work for George and Suzi." The auditors said they'd never seen this kind of warmth and loyalty in any other company.

After *Alice*, there was no more cold calling. Every studio called us. They still do.

I found the process for creating collections based on movies so fascinating and rewarding. For me the best part was getting the storyboards and seeing preliminary clips from the movie. There I could see the gist of the plot and the cast of characters—and I could catch a glimpse into the fictional world and see its predominant colors. I've drawn inspiration from characters' clothing, the color of key set pieces and props, or the colors from a landscape. Take *Shrek*, for example. The lacquer Who the Shrek Are You? is Shrek's exact shade of green, for example, and Fiercely Fiona is a green-tinged yellow that pairs perfectly with Shrek's hue. After that collection, DreamWorks CEO Jeffrey Katzenberg wrote to thank me for "bringing fashion to the swamp."

Working with movie studios provided a natural segue into working with celebrity brand ambassadors, a trend OPI started that has proved very successful. We've now created exclusive collections with a number of celebrity A-listers. Global megastars Justin Bieber and Katy Perry were among the first. Justin collaborated with our Nicole by OPI brand in 2010 for his exclusive One Less Lonely Heart collection. Nicole by OPI, named after George Schaeffer's daughter, is aimed at women eighteen to thirty-nine years old. Hip, trendy, and fashionable, we launched this line because customers in this demographic told us they wanted to buy OPI where they already shopped—from large chains like Target and Walmart or even their corner drugstore, for example. This partnership surprised a lot of people because we used a male spokesperson for a beauty brand, but it was massively successful. Justin's collection topped more than one million units sold within weeks of its release.

Katy Perry's 2011 collection, meanwhile, was released with the traditional OPI Nail Lacquer brand and featured lacquers named after songs from her chart-topping album *Teenage Dream*. This collection was the first to include a lacquer with the Shatter effect, which allowed users to create a black crackle effect on top of other colors. People went wild for Shatter—we couldn't keep it in stock.

Celebrity collaborations were so successful and so much fun for our fans that they've become a hallmark of our brand. OPI has created exclusive collections with such stars as Nicki Minaj, Selena Gomez, Mariah Carey, Gwen Stefani, Carrie Underwood, Serena Williams, Kerry Washington, and Pyper America. We don't limit ourselves to flesh-and-blood stars, either—everyone's favorite Muppet diva and fashionista, Miss Piggy, got her own mini-collection called Simply Moi! I consider myself very, very lucky to have worked with so many top celebrities who genuinely love nails and who've been happy to make time in their busy schedules to do photo shoots and speak on OPI's behalf and participate in promoting collections. I've had a great experience with each one.

We've also done collections based on stars of the small screen. *Keeping Up with the Kardashians* was a natural fit, as the entire Kardashian and Jenner clan are known for their trendsetting fashions, their beauty, and their megawatt star power. For the Nicole by OPI Kardashian Kolors collection, I designed colors inspired by each of these amazing women. It included such lacquers as Kendall on the Katwalk, Hard Kourt Fashionista, and Kim-pletely in Love. I also did a limited-edition Nicole by OPI Gossip Girl collection to coincide with the release of *Gossip Girl*'s third season on DVD, which included

GG-inspired names such as Party in the Penthouse and Too Rich for You. Partnering with the television show *Modern Family* was a less obvious collaboration, but it's a favorite show at OPI, and I loved designing colors based on these hilarious characters.

We also partnered with stars from the sports world, which produced some of my very favorite collaborations and campaigns. Working with tennis champion Serena Williams has been one of the highlights of my career. OPI teamed up with her for an exclusive Grand Slam collection—we released a mini-collection to coincide with each of the four major tennis tournaments of the year. This was one of my very favorite celebrity collaborations because in addition to being a record-smashing, world-class tennis player, Serena is a wonderful person and a terrific role model—and a certified nail technician. With her enthusiasm and technical knowledge, she was the most involved in the creative process of any brand ambassador I've ever worked with, and I can now say I've had the singular experience of having Serena Williams do my nails! Part of this collaboration involved Serena's famous appearance on *The Oprah Winfrey Show*, when she gave Oprah a pedicure using OPI products. At the end of the show, we worked with Oprah to do one of her legendary audience giveaways: the entire audience was treated to a manicure done by OPI professional nail technicians.

Serena and I have developed an ongoing friendship, and when my family had her over for dinner one night, she spoke to my kids about the hardships she'd gone through as a child, how she had to practice at 5 a.m. every morning and had missed out on so many of the things children enjoy. I remember saying to her, "Just keep talking, just keep talking." We were all so captivated by her story and deeply impressed by how even with her obvious natural talent, she had to work very hard to get to the top.

OPI's 2012 Endurance campaign, which was released in support of our groundbreaking GelColor system, featured powerful US women athletes who are all champions in their fields. Serena took part, as did gymnast Gabby Douglas, who brought home Olympic gold, trailblazing NASCAR champion driver Danica Patrick, and Olympic gold medalist volleyball player Misty May-Treanor. The campaign ad imagery featured these women at the top of their games—Serena powerfully slamming the ball, Gabby deftly defying gravity, Danica looking fast and fabulous behind the wheel, and Misty diving across the sand for the volleyball. This was one of my favorite campaigns because it highlighted the strength and fortitude of women, which was an inspiration for women and girls everywhere. It was the perfect match for OPI.

In just a few short years, OPI took nails from BARE TO THERE and made them a must-have element for an overall look.

As we established ourselves as a favorite of celebrities, and as we are ideally located in Hollywood, land of everyone trying to make it big, OPI became the celebrity and studio go-to brand. When stars needed red-carpet looks, their stylists came to us. Before OPI, nails were overlooked as part of an overall ensemble. But in just a few short years, nails went from BARE to THERE. Fashionistas and fashion writers the world over study every part of a model or a celebrity's look—hair, makeup, clothes, nails—and their observations get widely reported throughout the media and buzzed about online by fans. We've provided lacquers for untold numbers of red-carpet and runway appearances, as well as for movie and television sets, commercials, and music videos.

Often, we work with individual designers and houses of design, including BCBG, Hérve Léger, Charlotte Ronson, Jason Wu, Marc Jacobs, Rodarte, Jeremy Scott, and Rebecca Taylor. Designers will send me their full fabric palette along with actual swatches, and then I'll recommend colors that complement that season's collection. Our nail techs work on site to complete the final look. Or sometimes, OPI will do nail art designs based on a collection. Just to cite one example, in 2010 I teamed up with Zac Posen to create runway-ready looks finished with OPI nails. Zac was extremely involved in the process and very passionate about nails. He worked closely with us to design leopard-stamped, tie-dyed, and French nail (complete with moons) designs that complemented his incredibly colorful collection.

Another memorable experience was collaborating with the Miss Universe pageant for the 2013 Miss Universe Collection. Miss Universe 2010, Mexico's Ximena Navarrete, joined us to help promote the launch, and we did a photo shoot with her at the OPI campus. She was extremely gracious and kind and went through the entire factory giving hugs and speaking to all the employees. Fully 95 percent of our factory workers were from Latin America, so they were *super*fans of Ximena's. Production nearly came to a halt as we had people lining up to pose for pictures with her. (For a while, everyone's screen saver was a selfie with Ximena.) And as if from a slapstick comedy, we even had guys bumping into boxes and dropping things, so distracted were they by beautiful Ximena. At the end of her visit, Randy, head of production, came over to me brandishing a report and said, "Look, Miss Suzi! Two days! We lost *two days* of production." But it was all worth it. Ximena was the best, and we came away with a photo of the two of us—me in clogs and her Miss Universe sash, she in couture and two feet taller—that everyone at OPI got a good laugh over.

In short, we did it all, and we became known as the "never a no" company. That was the nature of this business—you had to move quickly because if you didn't, someone else would. We'd work with anyone in fashion and film and beauty, and no matter how challenging the request, we would come through, no matter what. Need a collection delivered to the set of *Friends* by the end of the day? Done. Get a color to a movie set in New York by noon? Done. Did

> *OPI became known as the "never a no" company. Need a collection delivered to the set of Friends by end of day? Done. Need a lacquer on a movie set in NYC by noon? Done. You name it, WE GOT IT DONE.*

a celebrity have a last-minute event and need a lacquer ASAP? We could do it. All of this work with the film, music, and television industries and with stars and their stylists solidified OPI's reputation as a red-carpet and celebrity favorite.

I can't say it was all glamorous, however. For *Skyfall* starring Daniel Craig, I did an OPI Skyfall collection with lacquers named after many of the iconic Bond movies. The studio was very pleased because this partnership helped bring in a female audience. They flew Harris and me to London for the premiere, which was attended by many celebrities, including Prince Charles and Camilla Parker Bowles. I loved this collaboration and was absolutely vibrating with excitement—but also with adrenaline and caffeine. As usual I'd worked right up until the very last minute, and as usual I'd overindulged in coffee. By the time Harris and I made it down the red carpet and to our box seats—where I was tottering about in four-inch heels that were killing me—I found myself on the verge of a panic attack.

I white-knuckled it through as much of the movie as I could, trying to practice deep breathing and not scream. But by the time the scene of M's death rolled around, my heart was hammering and I could barely breathe and I was convinced I was dying, too. I turned to Harris for help—and saw immediately that he'd be utterly useless. Harris Shepard is the world's biggest Judi Dench fan, and there he sat, wracked with heaving sobs. In my hour of need, my loyal companion, my right-hand man of twenty years, had come completely undone over a fictional character.

"*Fuck*, Harris!" I whisper-screamed. "I am having a *heart attack*! Stop *weeping*!"

That brought my loyal companion to his senses. Harris mopped his face and rushed me out of the theater, where I barely made it to the curb in my impossible heels. We'd left in such haste that Harris accidentally left his coat behind. He called our car service and told them to hurry—it was freezing out and I was still panicky and gasping for air. To our deep dismay, every black Mercedes that whizzed by was not ours. I felt bad for Harris so I gave him my short fur jacket, which he wound around his neck like a scarf. So there we stood, me in a sleeveless dress and impossible heels, Harris in his shirtsleeves and a makeshift scarf, both of us shaking from cold and anxiety, and sad we were missing the movie.

After an eon *our* black Mercedes finally arrived, and it whisked us back to the hotel, where Harris contemplated M's death and I had a nightcap and collapsed into bed. Tomorrow would be another day, and we would be in another country.

— eight —

LINCOLN PARK
AFTER DARK

M Y VERY FIRST EXPERIENCE OF NAIL POLISH WAS PAINTING
my mother's nails. This must have been a year or
two after we moved to America. Nail polish was rare in
Hungary when I was a girl, and Miriam and I wouldn't
be allowed to wear it until we were at least sixteen anyway. But I remember sitting at the kitchen table in our
apartment in Queens, painting my mother's nails a pale,
pearly pink. All nail polish struck me as such a luxury,
but at that point in my young life, this delicate shimmery
color seemed to me the height of elegance. Years later,

my mother and her love of pearlized colors would inspire Kyoto Pearl, one of OPI's most popular shades.

I have been drawn to color as long as I can remember. In Hungary, when we all wore the same drab school uniforms and few people owned objects whose sole function was beauty, my eye was drawn irresistibly to any instance of color. Maybe it was a flower pushing through a crack in the sidewalk or a clutch of wild peonies, or maybe it was the flash of color on a scarf worn by a traveler, or maybe it was a cobalt sky just after a thunderstorm. The rare times we were able to get fresh oranges,

I have always been drawn to color. For me color is BEAUTY, FREEDOM, PASSION, POSSIBILITY, SELF-EXPRESSION, and JOY all rolled into one.

I was as excited to gaze upon the vibrant orange of the peel as I was to eat them. Anything colorful could catch my eye and transport me—suddenly I was in a field of sunflowers, or in the Swiss Alps, or in a fragrant orange grove in some warm, faraway land. And though my outer circumstances hadn't yet changed, my mood and my outlook were entirely different from having encountered the beauty of color.

After we emigrated to Israel, with its towering palm trees and emerald terraces, all surrounded by the deep blue Mediterranean, I felt as if I were bursting into an entire universe of color. The colorful clothing was a revelation all on its own. Then multiply all of that color and freedom of expression a thousand times over when I arrived in one of the fashion and art capitals of the world, New

York City, where absolutely anything goes! Now that I've traveled extensively and have the ability to bring color into my life as I please, whether it's through fashion, art, interior design (or yes, fresh fruit, which I still don't take for granted), I still feel the same glimmer of possibility and freedom when I encounter color.

There are innumerable stories about the human obsession with color; our passion for it is deep and ingrained. We immerse ourselves in color in every aspect of our lives, from technology to home decorating, from fashion to beauty. And this isn't just a matter of aesthetics. Thinkers from Plato to Einstein to contemporary neuroscientists have studied the importance of color in our daily lives. From biological reactions that ensure survival, such as knowing when food is ripe or being aware of the changing of the seasons, to psychological reactions that affect blood pressure and heart rate, color influences our brain waves, our moods, and our parasympathetic nervous system. I once read an article in *Women's Wear Daily* that put it this way: "No matter who you are, where or how you live, or your physical, mental or spiritual requirements, the importance of color and the power it has within your daily life cannot be underestimated. A fundamental element to the human experience, color is the visual cue that draws us in to feel a connection with our environment and the things we love."

> *COLOR CAN TRANSPORT YOU. It can lift your mood, enliven your spirits, boost your confidence, and show you the possibility of something better.*

Color has immense power. It can transport you to a better place, even if you never leave your home. It can lift your mood, enliven your spirits, boost your confidence, and show you the possibility of something better. It can even light the way to freedom. Color can empower you to imagine and do and be more than you ever suspected possible.

And I saw that if I could capture all of that in nail color—if I could communicate its transformational power and make nail color relevant and special—I knew the world would embrace it as never before.

That, at root, is what OPI is all about.

Hot & Spicy

From the time I first started dreaming of getting into the color business, I was committed to empowering and enhancing the lives of all women by giving them an unlimited means of self-expression through color. Ten nails have the ability to speak ten thousand words. A French manicure, with its pristine white tips and perfect pink prettiness, for example, says something altogether different than long, crimson talons filed to points, or short, squared-off nails decked out in spring green. Before OPI expanded the color palette, nail polish had a very limited vocabulary. As there were only a handful of hues, women had to settle for only a handful of messages—blushing bride, let's say, or sexy vamp. Now, with so many colors and textures and finishes to choose from—not to mention the exploding nail art trend—

there is absolutely no limit to what you can say with your nails. This may be OPI's most enduring contribution: we gave women both the tools *and* the permission to express themselves in any way they choose. There is nothing more empowering.

With our first collection in 1989, we became known as the company that did color. Little did I know that those original shades, revolutionary as they were, were just the beginning compared to what's available now. When I first started out I never dreamed that one day I'd be creating blues and greens, or that OPI would be at the forefront of technological advances that resulted in glitter and holographic lacquers, over-the-top finishes like Shatter, or a new generation of salon-applied, soak-off colored gels.

But of course, these innovations make perfect sense. Because I always saw nail color as not *just* nail polish but rather an accessory on par with fine clothing and handbags, OPI started from a more elevated position than most nail care companies, and we were more willing to take risks. We wanted to give every woman unlimited choice in how she expressed herself through color, and I considered it my personal mandate to break barriers and offer something surprising with each new collection. When it came to colors that were considered unconventional at the time—such as those blues, greens, or yellows, or later, ultra-dark or neon nails for the mainstream woman—we were sure to feature those shades in our advertising. Once the consumer saw a chic model sporting blue nails, suddenly that color made sense, and it became aspirational. Or perhaps the consumer saw how monochromatic clothing could be instantly dressed up and made more exciting by accessorizing with flashy neon nails or a glittery finish. We used advertising to introduce the consumer to more unconventional products and show them how they could work in their own lives—how they, too, could be the next "it" girl. Beauty editors would then write about the latest out-of-the-box color or finish from OPI, and voilà, it became a trend.

The end result is that the entire rainbow is available to women, and with it the potential to communicate any mood, feeling, aspiration, or message. Now, no color is taboo, not for any age or any occasion. It's not at all uncommon to see bright blue nails in the boardroom, or the inkiest ebony at an afternoon playdate. And while green or blue *lipstick* might still be frowned upon at the office, it's now perfectly acceptable to wear green nails to work—or blue, or black, or eye-piercing yellow, or anything that strikes your fancy! Today, anything goes. Feeling indecisive? You can wear one color on your fingers and another on your toes. You can mix and match. You can wear twenty different colors on your twenty nails. The entire world of beauty is enjoying an unprecedented time of freedom in self-expression, individual creativity, and personal choice.

Today in nails, NOTHING IS TABOO. There has never been so much opportunity for creativity and individual self-expression.

OPI has always pushed the envelope when it comes to nail trends, from colors to finishes and even to nail lengths and shapes. (My favorite shape is the "squoval," or square with rounded corners shape, because it will never go out of style and looks good on any nail length.) I've often been asked if I ever feared I'd run out of ideas or if I'd end up repeating myself with a color. The truthful answer? Every time! But that fear was my best friend. I was determined not to repeat myself and to make every year better than before, which inspired me to innovate, innovate, innovate. So, to this day, even after thousands of nail colors, I approach each new collection and each new shade as if I'm designing for the first time and I have one shot to get it right. The pressure is enormous, and the stakes couldn't be higher. But it always spurs me to imagine new things—new raw materials, a new texture, a new finish, or sometimes, that holy grail, a color that shakes up the industry and changes what's possible in nail color.

In 2005, OPI released a color that sparked a revolution in the industry. A deep, nearly black purple like the midnight sky, Lincoln Park After Dark rewrote the rules on nail color and permanently turned the tide as far as what women would wear on their nails. Before this lacquer hit the market, ultra-dark nails were associated exclusively with the Goth community—and mostly, with very young women with very long nails. But I'd noted how very dark colors were cropping up in trend books and on the runways in the early 2000s, and I believed it was only natural that the dark-color trend would extend to the next accessory, nails. By 2004 I was willing to bet that the world was ready for this bold, dramatic hue, and if there was one thing I knew I could trust, it was my instinct for color.

My bet paid off. Seemingly overnight, ultra-dark nails became the hottest new trend, and they were considered chic whenever and wherever, regardless of season or occasion. Lincoln Park After Dark also looked fantastic on any nail length, and in fact, many people preferred it on very short nails. There was something rebellious and even dangerous about it—yet it still telegraphed an aura of high fashion and luxury. After the *New York Times* covered the craze, suddenly everywhere you went you saw women with Lincoln Park After Dark on their fingers and toes, and they were women of all ages and backgrounds, wearing it for any occasion. Professional fortysomethings sported it in the boardroom and out on the town, their teenage daughters wore it to school and by the pool, and their grandmothers wore it on vacation or just as their go-to day-to-day shade. Lincoln Park After Dark is still one of our bestsellers and has joined the ranks of iconic colors such as I'm Not Really a Waitress, Cajun Shrimp, and Bubble Bath that millions of people instantly recognize and know by name.

In this case, early test results all came back positive— everyone at OPI was captivated by Lincoln Park After Dark. Even Bryan Stein paid it his highest compliment by deeming it "terrible" and then wearing it around the office for the next several days.

This was decidedly not the case with our next big game-changer, however.

Russian Navy, from our 2007 Russian collection, is a deep, dark navy, nearly indigo, but with a hint of red shimmer that gives it a beautiful depth and a pop of surprise. I fell in love with this color, but I got pushback from quite a few people at OPI. "Who's gonna wear navy blue?" they said.

This wasn't our first blue. The first was Oyster Blue Lagoon, a shimmery blue-tinged frost that had appeared as early as 1997, and the next was Blue Moon Lagoon, a holographic blue-green from Summer 2003. We'd released a few other blues throughout the mid-2000s, but Russian Navy—which I named as an homage to *The Hunt for Red October*, one of my favorite movies of all time— was definitely the darkest, boldest blue. The marketing and creative teams were not at all on board.

I was convinced it was going to be a big hit, however, so this was one of the rare times I got a categorical no from the OPI family and I overruled them. "It's true that no one has seen a blue like this," I said, "but we want to *set* the trends, not follow them. We need to go with this."

I think I WAS BORN WITH AN INVISIBLE SET OF ANTENNAE that are attuned to color. When a color pings the antennae, I know immediately it's a lacquer that wants to be created.

We did, and the reception was great. Fans and beauty editors loved it, and everyone kept talking about how amazing this blue was. Russian Navy has never left our list and remains a consistent bestseller.

It's nearly impossible to predict which colors will capture the public's imagination and become instant classics. But so many OPI lacquers are considered icons in nail color that I'm often asked how I'm able to anticipate so many trends and create so many best-selling colors. I don't know that I could ever answer completely, as there is a mysterious aspect of having an instinct for color that's unknown even to me.

Perhaps the best way I can describe it is that I have an invisible set of antennae that are attuned to color trends. As I have since childhood, I actively pay attention to color all around me—in street fashion, on social media, in magazines, even the paint of cars—but that mysterious aspect, where a color will suddenly "ping" the antennae, requires no effort. I can be eating in a restaurant or engaged in a conversation or sitting in a meeting or walking through a new city, and suddenly I'm interrupted by a color that demands my attention. (This used to cause quite the disruption as I ceased everything and tried to commit the color to memory, but these days I just take a shot with my smartphone.) In any event, something about a color will just captivate me, and I'll know it's a shade that wants to be created. Sometimes a color will literally make me catch my breath. When this happens, I just *know*. That's how I created all of the OPI lacquers that have become fan favorites and household names—colors like Bubble Bath, Cajun Shrimp, I'm Not Really a Waitress, Kyoto Pearl, Big Apple Red, Strawberry Margarita, Samoan Sand, My Chihuahua Bites!, You Don't Know Jacques!, and Malaga Wine.

The other color question I'm constantly asked—and the one I admit I've been avoiding—is which OPI lacquer is my favorite. As you can imagine, this is a little like being asked to pick a favorite child. It's impossible! It doesn't help that as far as color goes in general, there is no color I dislike, not even the ones most people deem ugly, such as chartreuse, drab browns and greens, or eye-scalding neons. My feeling is, the color spectrum would be diminished by the absence of even one hue. There is a color for every mood or occasion, however rare.

The best I can do in selecting my favorite OPI shade is to narrow it down to a category—and that's an easy choice. My favorite will always be a red. I have loved red nails all my life—they feel so Hollywood and glamorous to me. To try and pick a specific red is more difficult. I will always have a warm place in my heart for OPI Red, because it's the first red I ever created. I also love Big Apple Red because it's a gorgeous color and a poignant reminder of the city that gave me a new life.

But of course I'll always love I'm Not Really a Waitress. It's the perfect color, the perfect name. It's so well-known it's become part of the cultural lexicon. This iconic "look at me" red captures the whimsical side of OPI. In Hollywood, we were surrounded by celebrities and people who wanted to be celebrities, many of whom were working as servers and bartenders as they tried to break into the movie industry.

Though the entire rainbow is now at our fingertips, RED will always be THE CLASSIC NAIL COLOR. It remains the favorite of Hollywood, New York City, and Paris.

I'm Not Really a Waitress was a playful nod to our neighborhood, but it also spoke to anyone laboring for a dream. Maybe your dream is to be an artist but for the meantime you're working a corporate job. Or maybe you want to be a corporate VIP but you're currently in entry-level sales. The message we wanted to send is that you can be anything you want to be, and that dreams are worth pursuing. OPI could help by giving you a boost of confidence. Fans seemed to get it, and they loved the color. *Allure* magazine inducted I'm Not Really a Waitress into its Beauty Hall of Fame in 2011, after it won best nail polish nine times. It remains our most award-winning and best-selling color.

So there you have it: "Suzi's Picks" for her OPI Top Three. That's as close as I can get to a favorite.

OPI by Popular Vote

Fortunately no one has to settle for picking only a few favorites—and in fact, many informal surveys have found that the average woman owns two or three dozen nail polishes. Then there are plenty of nail polish fanatics who own *hundreds* of bottles. I myself own more than one thousand bottles, which I keep in a library in my North Hollywood office. (For those who are curious, I get a manicure once or sometimes twice a week—it is really the *only* time I'm able to switch my brain off and completely relax—and when I'm testing new lacquers, I wear a different color on each nail.)

Of all the beauty products, nail polish is most likely to be found at the top of the list when it comes to the number of units people own. Few people have two hundred eye shadows or two hundred blushes, for instance. Perhaps the closest runner-up is lipstick, but even so, the average woman is far more likely to own many more nail colors than lipsticks. I think this is partly because of the sheer variety of colors available. But I think it's also due to the unlimited potential for self-expression so many choices give us and the ability to change your entire look with just a few strokes of a brush. It's irresistible! You're able to achieve far more effects and communicate a much wider message through nail color than through any other beauty product—and in one small, affordable, easily transportable package.

The term "Lipstick Index" was coined to describe women's spending habits during the post-9/11 recession. During this economic downturn, women cut back on expensive items such as a new dress or shoes, but cosmetics sales actually *doubled*. (The same trend was seen during the Great Depression, when cosmetics sales increased by 25 percent.) Just a decade after 9/11, nail polish surpassed lipstick as the new economic indicator and the new beauty must-have, even in lean times.

The experience of BEAUTY and SELF-CONFIDENCE is so EMPOWERING you can't afford to go without it. Nail color is an easy, affordable, and effective means to bring that into your life.

It doesn't surprise me in the least that nails have become the newest—and I would say most exciting— affordable luxury. Women will always want to pamper themselves and feel beautiful. Nail color accomplishes all of this without breaking the bank and without a huge investment of time. The experience of beauty is so empowering you really can't afford to give it up. You are happier and more confident when you look good, better equipped to realize your unique potential and make a bigger, better impact in the world.

For me, it all goes back to that common denominator, *color*. If there's anything that unites OPI's hundreds of millions of fans and creates meaningful connections among them—people of vastly different backgrounds and ages and lifestyles from more than one hundred countries—it's their shared love of color. This is what I call the OPI Culture of Color, and it's kept the brand fresh and relevant and exciting even after more than thirty-seven years. I think of it as a club that anyone can belong to. It's about self-expression and individuality, and it crosses cultural, language, ethnic, and age boundaries. The language its members speak is the language of color, and the experience of using that color to express their styles and personalities is the experience that brings them together.

When my kids were nine and six, we went on a family vacation to a ranch in Colorado. This was a classic dude ranch, with horseback riding, camping (or "glamping" in my case, though this was before anyone knew that term), fly fishing, archery, and, as the kids kept saying, "REAL COWBOYS," though I must note that many of the wranglers were women. In any event, there we were in remote Colorado along with other families from all walks of life who hailed from many different places in the world. We were enjoying a fairly quiet vacation . . . until one day I happened to wear a jacket with the OPI logo on the back. A few of the women asked me about the jacket and where they could get one, and when they learned I was one of the OPI founders their jaws dropped. Within hours it seemed as if everyone at the ranch knew "the OPI lady" was there. The women, guests and staff of all ages and backgrounds, sought me out to tell me about their manicures and how many bottles of OPI lacquer they owned, and the men went crazy wondering who this woman was all the women were talking about. By the end of the week I was voted the most popular person on the ranch.

That was one of those moments I got an inkling of how big OPI and its Culture of Color were becoming. I couldn't believe that there on a remote ranch, so many women not only knew about OPI but they knew *a lot* about OPI. They knew the names of their favorite colors and collections, they had particular colors associated with significant memories (such as their own or their daughter's wedding), and they knew my name as well. Many of them already owned dozens of OPI lacquers, and their enthusiasm made new fans out of the women who weren't yet the nail polish fanatics they were. When I got home I sent one hundred bottles of OPI Nail Lacquer to the ranch as a thank-you.

As the years went on this kind of scenario became more common, but I've never ceased to be amazed at the wide range of people who love OPI. I've met OPI fanatics all over the world, from all walks of life. They could not be more different from each other, but their common traits are a love of color and a keen enthusiasm for using nail color for self-expression.

The OPI Culture of Color now crosses gender boundaries as well. Throughout the book I've spoken predominantly about women because for most of my career, I created with women in mind. But in the beauty industry trends and styles and customs are always changing, and now countless men are making regular manicures a part of their self-care routines as well. OPI's Matte Nail Envy is very popular among men looking for groomed nails with an invisible finish. As for colors, the guys tend to go for Lincoln Park After Dark and Black Onyx, but once again, anything goes, and I admire men who aren't afraid of color. I believe nail color will become more and more common for men, as modern beauty is erasing traditional boundaries of gender, age, race, and sexuality.

Certainly in this age of social media, beauty is becoming more of a performance, and looks are instantly shared across the globe. Each of us is a collage of different cultures, aesthetics, and influences drawn from many places and from different eras. Whoever we are and wherever we come from, our clothing, our accessories, and our nails speak volumes about who we are—and who we are becoming.

— nine —

THAT'S BERRY DARING

ALL BUSINESSES WANT TO KEEP GROWING, AND USUALLY
they do this by offering more products, by expanding
distribution, or by acquisition. But as we always wanted
to do things differently at OPI—we wanted our customers
on the edge of their seats, always wondering what we'd
come up with next—I kept mulling over new and unexpected ways to grow the brand. One of my long-term
goals for OPI was to transcend the boundaries of being
only a beauty brand and grow into a total lifestyle brand.
We wanted to be everywhere our customers were, and
this meant understanding their desires and connecting

with them through other brands and products they already loved and were passionate about.

This idea for cross-branding and building a brand that would become something larger than the sum of its parts occurred to me early on. If we were delivering the message that nail lacquer wasn't *just* a bottle of nail polish but a fashion accessory, then OPI could be not *just* a beauty brand but a lifestyle brand.

And though our brand was affordable, it was still aspirational—that was much of the point! My first Hermès scarf was a high school graduation gift from a French friend of my mother's. At eighteen I couldn't afford anything from Hermès, but this gift was my first amazing accessory and my entry into the world of high fashion. It gave me a taste of couture at a time I couldn't afford an entire outfit. Likewise, OPI could be the entry into high fashion for young women who were just starting to find their signature styles. Maybe they couldn't yet afford high-end things, but they could treat themselves to a luxurious beauty product that was part of a lifestyle brand.

And hopefully they'd keep coming back for more, as I did with my Hermès scarf. I bought one for myself in my late twenties, and then I never stopped. I started collecting Hermès scarves, and they became my signature accessory.

There was also a practical reason for my ever-present scarves. The one argument I never won with George Schaeffer was over the temperature in the office. He was always hot and kept the air conditioning on full blast. Meanwhile I was always freezing. All day long, he'd lower the temperature on the thermostat, and I'd go behind him and raise it. Back and forth, back and forth, until finally he put a lock on the thermostat. I resorted to wearing winter clothes in the office, including a beautiful scarf every day. I would never win that particular argument, but I did the best I could by responding with fashion.

In 2004, we got a big opportunity for a cross-branding collaboration when Ford Motor Company reached out to us. What would we think, they wondered, about teaming up to create a mini-collection of lacquers based upon the Mustang? I loved the idea. One of America's most iconic cars paired with America's number-one professional salon brand of nail lacquer—to me this partnership made perfect sense. And if our customers initially did a double take—what did a sports car have to do with a bottle of nail polish?—then so much the better! An unexpected partnership would invite intrigue and excitement. It would spark conversation, increase buzz. And it would bring brand recognition to both of our established customer bases.

Ford knew this, too, of course, and one of their aims in collaborating with OPI was to attract more female buyers. So after we agreed to a partnership I went into the lab and created three lacquers inspired by the legendary Ford Mustang. Revved Up & Red-y was a dark cherry red, You Make Me Vroom a bright, "hot-rod red," and Gone Platinum in 60 Seconds a gorgeous, cool silver. These were bold, head-turning colors that looked equally at home on nails as on Ford's most famous model. To further solidify the partnership, we featured the Mustang's trademark galloping pony logo on each bottle's cap. We advertised in women's magazines, and both Ford and OPI promoted the collection on our company websites.

The outcome? From 2004 to 2005, sales of the Mustang rose by thirty-one thousand, and in 2006, they reached the highest sales for that model's generation. Now, of course I can't claim that the upsurge was due solely to "the OPI effect"! But certainly it was a mutually beneficial partnership. Customers loved the mini-collection and it flew off the shelves, and it was such a successful collaboration that nearly a decade later, Ford came back and asked if I'd create a limited-edition collection in honor of the Mustang's fiftieth anniversary. This time, I built the collection around "Race Red," which was designed and named after the Mustang's most popular paint color. This 2014 collection also featured a blue, a white, a pink, a gold, and a black, all vibrant, Mustang-worthy shades with Mustang-themed names such as Queen of the Road and Angel with a Leadfoot. Later that year, we released a mini-collection "pony pack" of the four best-selling colors.

Not long after we wrapped up our first collaboration with Ford, I ran across an interesting article that, if memory serves, was called "Learning to Swim in the Global Market." Granted, this was back in the mid-2000s, but the article made several good points that still apply. The author tells the story of a scientist who separated an aquarium into two halves with a glass partition. On one side, he placed a number of small fish. On the other he placed a large predator fish. Immediately, the predator fish saw the small fish and dashed after them. Swimming at full speed, the predator smacked right into the glass partition. This happened several times, until he finally gave up. A few hours later, the scientist removed the glass partition, but the predator never attempted to cross to the other side again. It would have starved to death in the midst of plenty had the scientist not placed it in another tank where it was fed regularly.

There are lessons here for any businessperson. First, circumstances change—you can (and should) count on that. Second, it's entirely possible to starve to death in the midst of plenty. Third, obstacles are rarely permanent, but not attempting to move them or overcome them guarantees they'll be permanent problems. Fourth, your mind is the only limit to the size of your market.

Today, the biggest "aquarium" of all is the global market. There is a world of plenty available for everyone, if only you have the right tools to access it. In our case, our biggest and most powerful tool is the OPI brand name. Put another way, we tapped into the global world of plenty through successful branding, which was largely built upon unconventional ideas.

Branding, at its simplest, is making the common uncommon. Just take Starbucks as an example. Starbucks made the common cup of joe totally uncommon. They wanted to do coffee differently than everyone else, they wanted to do it better, and most of all, they wanted to make coffee an *experience*. OPI

Branding is all about making the common uncommon. Look for ways to elevate your product from an OBJECT to an EXPERIENCE.

did exactly these same things, and thus we made over common nail polish, which had been around for years, into OPI Nail Lacquer, a high-quality, full-color, luxurious experience. And when we accomplished *that*, we made nails into an essential fashion accessory rather than an occasional treat.

Our unexpected branding partnerships only made us all the more uncommon. Ford was just one of the brands OPI teamed up with. In 2006 we partnered with Whirlpool. Again, if you're wondering what on earth nail polish has to do with home appliances, that's part of the point. We were looking for fun, surprising, out-of-the-box collaborations that invited a second and third look. And if you scratch just beneath the surface, the collaboration isn't so incongruous—after all, many of the same people who bought high-quality appliances also got regular salon manicures. So we teamed up with Whirlpool, and I created two colors to mark the debut of Whirlpool's new dishwasher. To put our own distinctive spin on it (of course the pun is intended), I came up with whimsical, funny names: Rinse Charming and, even more ironic, I Don't Do Dishes. It was a win-win: each of our brands was exposed to new consumers we wouldn't necessarily have reached otherwise.

That's the whole point of such collaborations. In 2009 I teamed up with Paige Premium Denim (now known as PAIGE) to create the OPI Bright Pair collection— six bright, summer-fun colors formulated to match Paige Denim's designer jeans and shorts. When Harris and I went to New York City to meet with the press, this time we met with both beauty and fashion editors. The Paige collaboration produced a remarkable new cross-pollination between beauty and fashion in the media—fashion editors were writing about a beauty product, and beauty editors were writing about fashion.

That same year we did one of our biggest collaborations, with Dell Computers. As we were already known as a company that did out-of-the-box partnerships, Dell recognized a good opportunity to team up with us. More and more women were buying laptops, and they were using them not just at home but at school, at the office, at coffee shops, at libraries—wherever they went, in other words, which represented a fantastic marketing opportunity. Dell suspected that women would want to personalize their laptops just as they did their nails and the rest of their look. So they asked us about creating laptop covers in iconic OPI shades. We loved the idea, and we ended up doing laptop covers in twenty-six classic OPI colors. This was the first time Dell allowed another logo on their laptop, and the name of the OPI color was also featured on the side.

For this collaboration, I found myself addressing technology editors for the first time when I went on a huge stage with Dell's VP of global marketing and introduced this great collaboration. The partnership created a lot of buzz in part because it was surprising. (And when OPI and Dell co-sponsored a booth at the annual SXSW Festival that year, no one was more surprised than Dell when people stood in line for hours to get manicures from OPI nail techs! The same thing happened in Vegas at Dell's computer show, when developers and programmers and software engineers—mostly men, by the way—lined up to get their nails done.) The key piece our two companies banked on was the consumer's desire to showcase her individuality. The consumer got to personalize her product and make it relevant to her unique taste and style, just as she did her nails. Once again, the collaboration proved so successful we'd go on to work together again: when OPI implemented its computer giveaway program for employees' children, naturally we purchased computers from Dell.

As we moved into the 2010s, we continued to collaborate with companies that appealed to our fans, including Kellogg's, Electrolux, Ace Hardware and their Clark + Kensington line of paint, Hello Kitty!, and Coke. Some of these partnerships were driven by consumer demand, such as Ace Hardware. We received countless requests from people who wanted to paint their walls in OPI colors, so we teamed up with Ace's Clark + Kensington to make gallons of paint in the world's favorite OPI shades.

But perhaps our biggest corporate collaboration was with Coca-Cola. If we wanted to be a total lifestyle brand, to be everywhere our customers were, Coke was a natural choice. Coke is such an American icon, not to mention the world's favorite soft drink. The Coca-Cola trademark is recognized by 96 percent of the world's population, and Coke sells 1.8 billion bottles of Coke per day in more than two hundred countries. I could already see the colors I'd create . . . starting with that classic Coke red.

Harris and I loved the idea, so Harris called the Coca-Cola reps on a Friday morning and pitched it. By

Tuesday we were being escorted into a massive conference room at Coke's Atlanta headquarters.

There must have been a dozen or more executives there, from management, global marketing, legal, and creative, and for a moment I feared we were in over our heads—I hadn't brought a PowerPoint presentation or even a single handout. Nor had I prepared any notes. For several seconds I had a "holy shit" moment as I wondered if I'd made a grave error—and the old public-speaking anxiety began to stir. But I sat down, took a deep breath, and just told the OPI story, of how we'd started with nothing and how I'd created all those colors that made nail color relevant and exciting, and how we'd elevated and transformed the entire industry—and, like Coke, had become a household name. I spoke with genuine passion and conviction, and the room was mesmerized. I ended by saying how amazing it would be to pair women's favorite drink with their favorite nail color brand—Coca-Cola and OPI were both in the business of providing happiness in a bottle, after all.

Harris followed up with a sketched-out PR campaign—again, no notes, no visuals—and the minute we were done the team leader gave a quick scan of the room, got nods from everyone, and said, "We're in. Let's make this happen."

Later, there would be the usual reams of contracts to draw up and sign, but this multimillion-dollar campaign between two global icons was essentially a handshake deal. It was a huge coup for OPI, and it wouldn't have happened without passion, or without that sense of urgency that continually drove Harris and me to work not just harder but better, and to take risks. When I speak to young entrepreneurs or business students, I always stress the importance of being willing to take risks and of seizing opportunity when it arises.

Opportunity knocks on a daily basis. But sometimes you have to squint your eye and FIND OPPORTUNITIES THAT OTHERS MISS. No one ever became an industry disruptor or an icon by maintaining the status quo.

Poet T. S. Eliot said, "Only those who will risk going too far can possibly find out how far one can go." I don't believe in the saying "Opportunity only knocks once." I think it knocks on a daily basis! But it won't always be obvious. You must be willing to squint your eye and see opportunities that others don't, to be bold, and to generate opportunities no one has ever thought of.

What if we hadn't made the leap into film and television, or what if we'd been too timid to call up Coca-Cola? You only live once, and none of us has time to put off missing an opportunity because it hasn't been done before or avoid taking a risk because someone might think it's odd or even silly. No one ever became an industry-disrupting icon by maintaining the status quo.

It's in the Cloud

One of the biggest disruptors of the status quo—for companies, for commerce, for communication, for the very way we live—is the Internet. Consider for a moment that OPI became a nationally known brand well before Facebook and Instagram and Twitter—or even before email! Promotion and marketing in those days were a time-consuming, very personal affair. When we needed to connect with a distributor or a sales rep or a PR person, we picked up the phone. We also traveled all over the world to personally put bottles of lacquer into the hands of fashion editors and journalists and to promote the brand at trade shows and industry events.

And when customers wanted to get in touch with us, that, too, was a matter of picking up the phone—or writing letters. Before the Internet, mountains of mail arrived at the OPI offices. Every day we received letters requesting colors or making suggestions for lacquer names. Some people wrote to thank us for their favorite colors, and plenty of people included snapshots of their OPI manicures, especially if they'd worn OPI for a special event like a wedding or an engagement party. I believed that no letter should go unanswered, so every Friday afternoon, my assistant Pat and I would settle in to read and reply to our fan mail. It took a great deal of time, but we sent everyone a personal response, and we included a gift, usually a bottle of lacquer from the latest collection. This was all part of the personal connection that's part of the DNA of OPI—it's part of the lightning we caught in a bottle. We wanted communication to feel like a friend-to-friend discussion versus an impersonal company-to-consumer interaction, and that was our practice long before we all moved to digital media.

SOCIAL MEDIA represents a fundamental shift in the way business is conducted. It has turned ordinary word of mouth into extraordinary communication and connection.

Now with the Internet, and more specifically, social media, the relationships have moved online. Social media is not a fad. It represents a fundamental shift in the way we communicate and the way we find and buy products and follow trends, and in the way businesses promote and sell products. Social media has turned ordinary word of mouth into extraordinary communication and connection.

As will be no surprise to anyone, I may be the least tech-savvy person around. But when social media started to hit the scene, I saw immediately that it was all about personal connection. People were keeping in touch with friends and family—and they were making *new* connections as well. Lots and lots of them! I saw in this a huge opportunity for a company like OPI, which was built upon personal connections and relationships, and which created inherently sharable products. As the handwritten letters and snapshots attested, our consumers have always loved to be involved with the brand and to be part of the OPI story. Social media just made that interaction easier, faster, and vaster.

Now, consumers connect with us through their laptops and smartphones, and it takes no more than a few clicks. As you can imagine, Pat and I had to wave the white flag of surrender years ago—there was no way we could keep up with the deluge of online communications.

OPI now has a dedicated team of social media mavens that monitors our multiple platforms and interacts with fans. It's this real-time interaction that wins the love and loyalty of consumers, and it has allowed us to do so much more as a company. Through social media and our website we announce and promote new products, tell our story, provide

SOCIAL MEDIA HAS COMPLETELY MADE OVER THE BEAUTY AND FASHION INDUSTRIES. It's where the real dialogue is occurring, where the advertising is happening, where the trends are breaking—and where the fans are interacting with each other, with their favorite brands, and with their favorite brand ambassadors.

a place for fans to tell their stories, offer technical tips, hold contests and giveaways, organize charitable efforts, and get to know our customers in ways we never thought possible. One of the most popular features of our website is the interactive Try It On function, which allows users to see what the colors will look like on their own skin tone and their own nail length. The OPI Nail Studio app lets you upload photos of your own hands and get an even more realistic image when testing out colors.

Consumers will always want to interact personally with their brand—and social media actively encourages and facilitates it. Today's consumers want to be part of the unfolding drama of a product's development, to be part of the ongoing evolution of the company. They want to be as close to the action as possible, even to feel that they're on the team with the creators of the brands they love. In the past, consumers wanted industry experts and fashion insiders to advise them or alert them to the next breaking trend and provide tips on what to wear, buy, or use. Now, social media has elevated the *consumer* to a position of influence and authority. The consumer is now the author, the tastemaker, the influencer, even the marketing team.

This may be especially the case for Generation Z, the generation just after Millennials. Whereas other generations have had to adapt to the rise of social media and mobile technology, Generation Z was born into it. They are true digital natives. Any business hoping to connect with Gen Z—and trust me, we all need to—must understand who they are and how they are already becoming the next big disruptor in consumer goods marketing. Even though these consumers are still quite young, they are some eighty million strong and command $44 million in purchasing power. They represent the future of commerce, and certainly so for the ever-evolving, breaking-news-driven fashion and beauty industries.

OPI is already taking cues from Gen Z's desires for interacting with brands. So what you won't find on OPI social media platforms is any ad and campaign imagery. Gen Z doesn't passively absorb heroes and marketing hype, and they don't want Photoshopped, staged images. They'd rather see uniqueness, authenticity, spontaneity, and diversity represented than the polished images that previous marketers preferred. They want to see *themselves* and their peers in the picture, using the products in their own creative ways. So OPI obliges! We take the best images from our fans and followers and repost them. Everyone can be part of the story.

Our latest brand ambassador is Gen Z phenom Teyana Taylor, and I could not be more excited about the newest face of OPI. Teyana and her team at her '90s-themed OPI-concept salon Junie Bee Nails in Harlem are doing some of the most exciting and innovative nail art in the industry. Like many stars of her generation, Teyana is gifted in multiple areas of entertainment—recording artist, songwriter, actor, dancer—and adeptly leverages social media to showcase her immense talents. She can now add salon owner to her list of accomplishments. Check out her Junie Bee Nails Instagram account to see what's happening in nails at this Harlem hotspot.

Social media has completely made over the way the beauty and fashion industries operate. This is where the real dialogue is occurring; this is where the advertising is happening; and this is where the trends are bubbling up and breaking. Now, you don't exist without social media, and businesses can seriously change the conversation from "return on investment" to "return on relationship."

Social media has flattened the distance between celebrities and fans, between designers and customers, between tastemakers and consumers. It offers a 24/7 source of inspiration and information and has fed the globalization of beauty. In an instant, consumers can spot trends happening anywhere in the world. And when they see it, they want it. Not next month or next week—they want it NOW. Social media is *in the moment*. With just a few moments' scrolling, a consumer can understand the culture of a brand and connect with the brand (or not) on an emotional level. Even though the world is now in an I-want-it-now digital age that operates on a global stage, consumers still rely on personal interaction and still want to feel that a brand is invested in them. Emotional connection to a brand engenders more than fleeting interest and a few quick clicks.

And not to put too fine a point on it, but obviously, consumers can now *buy* very quickly—just look at Amazon's 1-Click purchasing option as one example. People buy things they connect to emotionally, and women the world over connect emotionally with color and nail lacquer.

To Infinity and Blue-yond

Thanks to social media, one of the most incredible things I've witnessed in the past decade is the extraordinary creativity and enthusiasm of OPI's fans. They are an active, powerful, and innovative community. They adore being a part of the OPI story and interacting with anyone else who uses OPI products, from celebrities to nail artists to salon owners to everyday fans. In effect they have become our volunteer brand ambassadors. And there are a lot of them!

Enjoying what OPI fans are sharing is, I will admit, largely the extent of my social media use. I do look at Twitter for news, and I have Facebook and Instagram accounts but I never post anything. Honestly, I'm pretty clueless when it comes to this stuff, and I much prefer to use social media to see what's going on in fashion and

beauty. But I adore watching YouTube videos of nail artists at work—one of my favorites is the eminently gifted
celebrity nail artist and OPI ambassador Tom Bachik—
and I absolutely love to see how fans around the world
are using OPI lacquers. I love that they feel part of the
OPI story, and that they can interact with celebrities,
nail artists, or everyday fans. This ability to interact and
in effect co-create with us has helped inspire deep love
and loyalty of the OPI brand and has made us that much
more relatable. Any platform that allows users to share
photographs is the perfect medium for fans to share their
latest creations, and thus OPI has taken on all-new relevance with new generations in the age of Instagram and
Snapchat.

OPI fans also love to get in on the action in the
lead-up to the release of any new OPI collection. The
online buzz is positively electric as fans all over the world
gleefully anticipate the latest colors and wonder together,
What has OPI come up with this time? Then, literally within
hours of the release, fans are blogging, vlogging, tweeting,
updating, and sharing reviews and photographs. This is
the worldwide OPI Culture of Color at work, and once
again, it's all about relationships and having an emotional
connection to the brand. OPI fans in even the most far-
flung places have been able to connect and form relationships based upon their shared love of color. On our social
media platforms and on fans' blogs and websites, language
barriers recede before the universal languages of color and
snapshots and emojis, and the boundaries of distance and
age simply don't exist.

But the enthusiasm doesn't stop with sharing photos of manis, pedis, and nail art, incredible as that is. OPI fans love to come up with innovative ways to use our nail lacquer. They host themed parties based on lacquers, such as "Chick Flick Cherry" for movie night or "Be There in a Prosecco" for cocktail parties. They give OPI Lacquer as party favors or include bottles in gift bags, which is easy to do when there is an aptly named lacquer for every significant milestone in life—engagements, weddings, pregnancies, births, graduations, promotions, retirements, even breakups and funerals. OPI fans have painted their cars and their motorcycles and their walls in OPI shades. They post photos of their destination-collection manicures when they visit that country. They have used lacquers to help them propose, make an announcement, or mark landing—or leaving—a job, and they share all of these incredible ideas on social media. I'm still amazed that strangers all over the world reach out every single day and say *Look how I used OPI Nail Lacquer, look what I did with this color!* They took OPI products and ran with them and expanded their use in ways we never could have anticipated.

It's deeply meaningful to me when fans share how OPI played a part in some of their most cherished memories—or helped them navigate difficult times. One of my favorites was the female F-16 fighter pilots serving in Afghanistan who sent us photographs of their team showing off their OPI nails. When we heard about these amazing women who were so capably serving our country, we sent them a shipment of nail lacquers to help bring a little light and levity into their lives. We also got so many letters and emails from people who were grappling with illness or who were undergoing chemotherapy or radiation, and many times we heard from patient-advocate organizations as well. We'd send nail techs to hospitals or to these organizations' events to bring a little cheer into patients' lives and help them feel more feminine and attractive. Or once a month we'd send nail techs to a local kidney dialysis center and provide manicures while patients sat for hours receiving treatment. These are the meaningful moments when OPI could easily step in and bring a little happiness and beauty into the lives of people who were experiencing hardship. The nail techs loved to help in this way whenever they could.

I always wanted to create a brand that was present wherever our customers were, that was able to connect with them and help them mark the occasions of all their most memorable moments or help them get through their most difficult times. I can truthfully say that that has happened, and I'm so grateful for it—but it's not I who can take the credit! That goes to the legions of OPI fans, the global OPI Culture of Color, the most loving and loyal fans in the world.

ten

PURPLE WITH A PURPOSE

Y OU GIVE, YOU GET.

This is what my father always said. He didn't mean you give *in order* to get. Instead he was acknowledging the truth that there is a natural rhythm to things—acts of generosity go out into the world and sow more acts of generosity. Sometimes, you will be the one bestowing the generosity. And sometimes, you will be the one receiving it.

Of course, the opposite is also true. Not giving— saying no when you have the means to help—sows selfishness. No one is helped, including yourself.

The truth is, none of us gets through life on our own. Not a single one of us would be where we are without the risk and sacrifices, and the acts of kindness and generosity, of the people who have gone before us. Before we even had children, my husband George and I agreed that it is important to teach kids from a young age to be involved in charitable giving. They can donate a portion of their allowance to a charity of their choice, give back to their schools with volunteer hours, or get involved in local fund-raising efforts or food drives, for example. These things teach them discipline, budgeting, *and* kindness. We also required that our children donate part of their bar and bat mitzvah money to a good cause, and we left it up to them to research and choose the charity.

> *NO ONE GETS THROUGH LIFE ALONE. We will all be the recipients of others' generosity from time to time, and we should remain on the lookout for opportunities to pay it forward.*

And though the other George in my life, George Schaeffer, and I could bicker like siblings, we were likewise always in full agreement regarding our profound gratitude and our obligation to give back. As children of Holocaust survivors and as immigrants who had come to America seeking better opportunities, we were keenly aware of what we'd been given, and we felt a deep responsibility to give back in return.

Thus philanthropy is built into the heart and soul and spirit of OPI. We look on charitable giving as a moral obligation—but not as a burden. On the contrary it is a delight and a privilege to be able to give back some measure of what we have received, and to make a difference in the world. As Winston Churchill said, "We make a living by what we get, but we make a life by what we give."

Worth a Pretty Penne

I believe that charitable giving is important for every business, no matter its size. Businesses prosper when their employees band together around a common cause. Yes, the purpose of a business is to provide products and services for customers and a livelihood for employees— businesses want to make money. But giving back some of those profits unites employees in something bigger than themselves and imbues them with a sense of purpose. If you want employees whose enthusiasm runs far deeper than impacting your bottom line, get your company involved in charitable giving.

Choosing your charitable organizations is half the fun and goes a long way in demonstrating your company culture. At OPI, because our overall commitment in whatever we do was to empower and enhance the lives of women, our charitable efforts have focused on organizations and movements that support causes near and dear to women's hearts, such as women's health, education, and anti-violence. We've supported breast cancer, diabetes, heart disease, and leukemia research; beauty treatments for women receiving cancer therapies; anti-bullying initiatives; scholarship and after-school programs; and local community efforts to fight hunger. We have given money and donated OPI products, but we also donated our time and energy in the form of participating in fund-raising walks like the Susan G. Komen Race for the Cure, volunteering at food pantries, hosting bone marrow and blood drives on the OPI campus, collecting food and clothing for low-income families in the Los Angeles area, and volunteering in after-school programs at L.A. elementary schools.

Perhaps best of all, through our platform we were able to bring global exposure to the charities that are relevant to our customers' lives—and we were able to provide a fun, beauty-filled way to get them involved. The Pink of Hearts promotions, for example, offered limited-edition pink lacquers in support of breast cancer research. Money from the sales of those colors went to the Susan G. Komen foundation for breast cancer research, so when women purchased them they were also supporting scientific research that directly impacted them or their loved ones. It's been such an honor to make these sorts of connections happen and to use OPI to make a positive difference in the world.

Social media has made charitable giving and getting our customers involved easier than ever. One of our latest campaigns was a partnership between OPI and The Little Market, a nonprofit online fair-trade shop that features the work of female artisans. The Little Market's mission to empower women and help women improve the quality of life in their own communities aligns perfectly with ours. So through social media we sponsored a giveaway contest that would appeal to our consumers.

Once again, it's two organizations, coming together to increase awareness and to bring in more dollars—for business and for charity.

Corporate charitable giving can also help attract and retain top employees. Millennials, the largest section of the American workforce, are highly socially conscious and have led the charge in insisting on work environments that reflect their values. They want their work to be meaningful and to make a difference in the world. Your company's charitable giving program is a significant part of an overall package that demonstrates its values and its priorities. Employees look for companies that share their values—and they remain loyal to those companies.

The same is true for consumers. More than ever before, customers "vote" with their dollars. If a company is engaging in practices that customers deem unethical, they'll simply take their business elsewhere. On the other hand, if a company shares their values and supports causes they believe in, consumers will consistently choose that product—even if others are less expensive or more convenient to purchase.

Your company's philanthropic efforts, no matter how large or small, also reflect the values of its leadership. I've always tried to lead by example, so I've made a conscious effort to be kind and charitable while at the same time being focused on making our business a force for the greater good. There are many thousands of people relying on our success, and I believe we are here for the sake of others. No matter how big a business gets, one cannot forget to care about and listen to the people who contributed to making it so. So, as the saying goes, "Charity begins at home."

Finally, philanthropy makes you a good neighbor. While I'm all for supporting large charitable organizations that help millions of people, I also think it's vitally important to help the people right there in your own community. It's a civic responsibility, and it promotes a positive relationship between your business and your community. You invest in your community when you work to improve it. And don't forget that if you *don't* get involved with your own community it can have negative repercussions—the company with a "don't care" reputation won't keep its employees or its customers and won't win the respect of its neighbors.

I've mentioned that every Friday my assistant Pat and I would go through the letters people sent to OPI. Much of it was fan mail, but we regularly received requests from local people asking for support. Businesses, charities, churches, mosques, synagogues, community groups, centers for the elderly, youth services organizations, food pantries, homeless shelters . . . you name it. We always wrote back and we always included some sort of gift or contribution. Other requests were about time and learning resources. Once, a local middle school contacted us about working with their science classes. Because we were right there in the neighborhood, they wanted to do a project on nail lacquer, testing it to see how and why it stayed on, how long it took to dry, and so on. Of course we said yes, and we sent our R&D team out to partner with the students to conduct their experiments.

We also received many letters from people who wrote to us simply to share the troubles they were experiencing—illness, the loss of a job, the loss of a loved one, loneliness. These letters touched me deeply. There was so much sadness in the world, so much illness and suffering—I felt the least we could do was respond with a handwritten note and a small gift of the latest lacquer or lotion. One young man whose mother was diagnosed with terminal cancer reached out to us. During her final weeks he was constantly by her bedside, and even then she insisted that her nails be adorned in her signature color, OPI Red. He was writing to thank us for "always making my mom feel special." We ended up naming a color after him and donated all the proceeds to a foundation he established for his mother. This is the sort of thing that would happen more often than you'd think at OPI. Consumers love a personal connection between themselves and their favorite companies, and I'm so happy our fans felt such a connection that they trusted us with their stories.

I'm just as happy that as we grew and became more profitable, we were able to increase our charitable giving and expand our ability to make a positive change in the world.

Reach for the Sky

I cannot leave a discussion of giving back without mentioning my mother, Magda Weiss, who is the finest example of generosity and the triumph of the human spirit

I've ever known. She is as much a part of OPI as George Schaeffer or me or any of our employees, and nowhere is her example more present and more enduring than in OPI's philanthropic practices.

As I've mentioned, observant Jews are raised practicing *tzedakah*, or charitable giving. *Tzedakah* includes acts of charity such as donating money to the cause of your choice or dropping off canned goods at your local food pantry, but it's so much more than this. It's a way of being in the world, an overall spirit of compassion and generosity. And it's this quality that my mother instilled in me, by overt lessons, yes, but more so by the way she lived, which is all the more remarkable given what she endured in the Holocaust.

I would not understand the full tragedy of my mother's story until 2005, when my mother, my niece Nicole, my sister Miriam, and I made a visit to Auschwitz. My mother had been begging to go back. At first we dissuaded her. We were afraid of how she'd react, and because she was already in her eighties, we knew the trip would be difficult. Her physician said we would have to be careful. But she was persistent, and finally we arranged to go.

When we finally arrived at Auschwitz's infamous wrought-iron entrance gate, with its foreboding slogan *Arbeit macht frei* ("Work sets you free"), my eighty-two-year-old mother shocked everyone when she slipped past the crowd and took off running, deep into the camp. We called to her to slow down, that there was no need to hurry or run. But she ran. Not *away* from the horrors she'd experienced in that awful place, but directly toward them. She ran as if she knew exactly where to go, and we pushed through the crowds to follow her. We found her on her knees by the gas chamber where her mother and brothers had been killed, saying *Kaddish*. She bent low, head to the rubble, as if to feel them. It had been her life-long dream to pray this ancient Hebrew mourner's prayer for the family that had been taken from her.

Back at home—our lives of comfort and love in sunny Southern California providing a study in contrasts if there ever was one—my mother began to speak. She told us how she and her mother and her two younger brothers had been herded onto cattle cars and transported to Auschwitz. As soon as they arrived they were separated, and she never saw them again. Her mother, too old to work, and her younger brothers, too young to work, were sent to the gas chamber immediately.

She alone was spared. Every morning, my mother and her cohort were given black coffee and a stimulant. That was breakfast. Then they were sent to work in the fields until sundown. There was no lunch, and for the evening meal they were given soup, which was mostly broth. Every few days, someone could get lucky and receive a gristly piece of meat or perhaps a potato in their evening broth. Once, my mother was lucky enough to find a raw potato on the ground, and at great risk, she hid it in her sleeve. After nightfall she nibbled on it bit by bit, making it last, and shared some with her bunkmate.

For one year she labored in that death camp, witnessing unspeakable atrocities. Workers who collapsed from exhaustion or illness were immediately shot, as a warning to all. My mother also recalled a cruel game the Nazis would play: after rounding up the starving workers, a guard would throw food on the ground before them. Any person who scrambled to the ground in a desperate lunge for sustenance was shot immediately.

My mother is ninety-four now. Though she is feeble and suffering from progressive dementia, she is never without a smile. Sometimes I'll find that she's hidden an object in her sleeve. She confides that it's a potato and asks me not to tell anyone, because she will need it for later.

In the face of all this, it's remarkable, perhaps even a miracle, that my mother is so loving and joyful and generous. When this is part of your family history, and when your mother sets this kind of example, how could you not give back? My mother is my hero, and I believe my own success is merely a reflection of who she is. I give back in honor of her and my father.

And in honor of America. It was the Americans who liberated the camp where my mother was imprisoned. It is America that welcomed two Hungarian immigrants and gave us the chance to build a new life for ourselves, our families, and our employees. Only in America is it possible to start with nothing other than a drive to succeed, a passion to better yourself, and a great idea, and make the desire for success a reality. We are living the American dream, and every day I am grateful to have been given this "great opera-tunity."

MY MOTHER IS MY HERO. My success is merely a reflection of who she is.

Living the American dream includes philanthropy. Gandhi famously said, "What is faith if it is not translated into action?" The act of giving back is a civic responsibility, and if you have been blessed with every form of abundance, as I have—health, happiness, family, wealth—I believe you have a moral responsibility to give back as well. I never take these things for granted, and I never forget how profoundly grateful I am. It's good to remember that every single one of us will be in need at some point. The ways in which we're "needy" will look very different from person to person and situation to situation, and different at different points in life. But each of us has been helped at some point along the way, and each of us will have the opportunity to help. You give, you get; you get, you give.

— eleven —

IT NEVER ENDS

WHAT MAKES A BRAND ICONIC?

Does that happen when you reach, say, a million dollars in sales? A million in profit? A billion? When you amass a certain number of social media followers? When you're all over the media, or the favorite of all the celebrities?

Those things may be traits of some, though not all, iconic brands, but they're not what makes a brand iconic.

The truth is, brands come and they go. Some don't even last a year, while others persist for decades and are considered successful by any standard business measure.

But the vast majority of even truly great brands don't achieve the status of icons. The icons are the cream of the crop, the brands that withstand the test of time and become a part of the cultural consciousness. These are the brands that don't follow trends but set them, the brands that are able to reinvent themselves so as to be fresh and new while still maintaining their original integrity. The true icons of the world have become household names. Apple. Nike. Gucci. Coca-Cola. Tiffany. What is it that makes these brands different from all the rest?

Iconic brands from any industry are far greater than the sum of their parts. They have become something bigger and more meaningful than their products' intended functions. You don't purchase a Tiffany lamp merely to illuminate a room, for example—any chain store lamp can fulfill that function. You buy Tiffany to participate in a storied tradition of beauty, elegance, handcrafted design, and luxury. So, while you're buying a beautiful lamp with a colorful stained-glass shade, you're also buying participation in the overall aura of the Tiffany brand. You are literally buying into the brand's mystique.

ICONIC BRANDS SUCH AS OPI HAVE BECOME FAR MORE THAN THE SUM OF THEIR PARTS. They are deeply embedded in the cultural consciousness and maintain a provocative and valued place in the wider culture.

Consumers the world over are readily able to perceive an iconic brand's unique aura, and they are willing to buy the brand's products in order to partake in it. The aura of an iconic brand touches everything in its path, from products to causes to relationships to cultural artifacts. An iconic brand has staked out a provocative and valued position in the wider culture. What we traditionally think of as the components of a brand—the name, the trademarked logo, the product's distinctive design features, its unique packaging—are simply markers that are empty and devoid of meaning without a history of cultural relevance. An iconic brand exists synergistically with all aspects of culture and society, and its aura has exerted such a dominant influence that the brand transcends the traditional bounds of its own particular category. That's why you don't have to be a tech aficionado to know that Apple makes superior computers and smartphones, or a sneaker enthusiast to know that Nike is one of the most successful brands of all time, of any product.

Likewise, even people who have never stepped foot into a nail salon know the brand name "OPI," and they know it stands for high-quality nail lacquer. And chances are, the minority that aren't personally familiar with OPI are only one layer removed from someone who is.

I was once at an editors' lunch at Le Bernardin in Manhattan. There were ten or twelve of us seated at a large round table, and as was usual for any OPI meeting, we were probably the loudest, most raucous group in the restaurant. All throughout lunch we were, as my son would say, laughing our asses off, and we attracted the (envious) attention of not a few diners. A man sitting nearby eventually asked us who we were and what was going on at our table. Well, what he said exactly was, "What the fuck is this OPI I keep hearing about? Apparently I'm in the wrong line of work!"

Over everyone's laughter I asked him if he had a wife or girlfriend. He said he had a wife, so I told him to call her and ask her what OPI was.

And he did! He left the dining area, and about ten minutes later he came back, eyes wide. "Oh my God!" he said. "My wife told me who you are. OPI is her favorite! And she said she always wears—wait a minute, am I getting this right? Yank My Doodle?"

As you can imagine, the whole table cracked up all over again. It's a wonder we didn't get kicked out of Le Bernardin that day.

Scenes like this have happened too many times for me to count. Everywhere I go, people are amazed and thrilled when they hear I have *any* association with OPI, and when they realize I'm the Suzi of such lacquers as Suzi Nails New Orleans or Suzi Shops & Island Hops, they're blown away. Let me emphasize that it's not *me* they're so carried away with—it's the brand. I think one thing we did very differently at OPI is that in addition to creating a company culture, we created a culture of the *brand*. The brand telegraphed luxury, excitement, and beauty, and it sparked devotion, trust, and love among its fans. They wanted to be a part of the brand's aura.

The OPI brand has now become so enormous, so widespread and recognizable. It's grown so much larger than the sum of its individual parts, so much larger than

George or I ever could have envisioned—and so much larger than any of us who worked at OPI could have orchestrated even with our best efforts. That's because it's the *consumers* who have taken up the baton and have voluntarily publicized OPI all over the world. The OPI aura has truly taken on a life of its own and has become something so much larger and more richly diverse and more beautiful than we alone could have authored. It is our fans who have made the brand an icon.

As odd as it sounds, it took moments like the ones at Le Bernardin for me to grasp how widely known and how pervasive in the marketplace OPI had become. I was always so deeply immersed in the work—constantly multitasking eight or ten or twelve hours a day—that it was only in moments like these that I could come up for air and catch a glimpse of what was happening "out there."

A couple of other such moments stick out in my mind. One occurred at home. My kids weren't impressed with what I had accomplished at OPI until they were older, because they always just knew me as "Mom," the person who showed up for carpool and family dinners. Plus they had never known me as anything other than a working mom, so to them OPI seemed like any other job. But once when Andrea had a slumber party with some junior-high classmates, her friends put two and two together and realized I was *the* Suzi who founded *the* OPI . . . and much high-pitched squealing ensued. (And you can bet they all got manicures.)

The other time I remember thinking, *Wow, this thing is huge—I've really made it!* occurred at none other than

Walmart. I traveled to Walmart's headquarters in Bentonville, Arkansas, to introduce the Nicole by OPI Kardashian Kolors collection. Our account salesperson and the VP of sales and marketing were also there, and I was so inordinately excited about this trip they thought I was crazy. But Walmart was the biggest retailer in America and certainly an icon in itself. To me it represented the brass ring of retail success—I felt I had truly made it in America and that OPI was a truly established brand if we were being sold at Walmart.

I never stopped being amazed at the response the letters O-P-I provoked. Everywhere I went—and I mean everywhere—if someone realized I was affiliated with OPI, they wanted to tell me about their nails and what color they were wearing. Many times, people want me to guess their lacquer shade, or they want to talk to me about their favorite colors and favorite names. (And I can't tell you how many times strangers have actually taken off their socks and shoes to show me their toenails.) It could be a server in a restaurant, a teacher or professor at a kid's school, another parent at a Little League game, a flight attendant, a librarian, a clerk at a store, a nurse, a doctor, a stylist, a Fortune 500 CEO. This is just an off-the-cuff sample of the people who have shown me their nails over the years. At a glance it illustrates how people from all walks of life love the OPI brand, which is another mark of an icon.

The other thing that has never ceased to amaze me is how often perfect strangers want to confide in me. I've already mentioned the handwritten letters people used to send us, sharing stories of illness, loss, and triumph. Now that happens online or in person. So many people will approach me after my public appearances and share personal stories. Sometimes these stories are related to OPI—women love to tell me what nail color they wore at their weddings or baby showers, for example—but sometimes they're not.

I admit that at first I was baffled as to why this was happening . . . until one day it hit me that it actually made perfect sense. For a company that had gone out of its way to establish a personal connection with its consumers, of course they felt that personal connection and acted on it! In other words, we had succeeded in establishing such a personal connection with our consumers that perfect strangers treated me like an old

OPI created an instant classic by connecting to women on an emotional level, by making nail color personal and relevant to women's lives, and by ELEVATING NAIL COLOR FROM A PRODUCT TO AN EXPERIENCE.

friend. It also didn't hurt that no matter how big my reputation as "Suzi the First Lady of Nails" became, I'm always just plain old Suzi Weiss-Fischmann. I'm the same person at home as I am at the office and as I am in my public appearances. I rarely stopped to think about how I was perceived (I was too busy), and I never took myself too seriously (life is too short not to laugh every day). I was just so happy that I was able to do the work I did as a career, my life's passion. I think people always pick up on and connect to that kind of enthusiasm and authenticity.

These are the kinds of responses the OPI brand inspires, which have everything to do with that personal connection we established. The minute we debuted our nail color line in 1989, OPI changed the way women perceived nail polish. We made nail color *personal* and *relevant* to women's lives, and we made nail color an *experience*. We invited women to participate with us on a journey that transported them to new, uncharted territories of color and beauty, and thus we appealed to and connected with our customer base on an emotional level. That's why our consumers became deeply invested in the brand quite quickly. And that's how we created an instant classic, a product that immediately prompted consumers to visit salons and ask for OPI by name.

But of course, no brand is an instant icon. Becoming an icon is a process that happens over time, and in fact, longevity is one of the hallmarks of an iconic brand. Icons have staying power. To stick around for the long term, they must continually remain relevant and exciting, and engage with the culture in new and unexpected ways. This is quite an extraordinary feat for fashion or beauty brands, which live and die based on the latest breaking trends. What's hot one season is definitely not hot the next! In our era of social media and the outsized role of online cultural influencers and tastemakers, a brand can be on top of the world one day and considered passé the next. OPI debuted as a brand to watch, but it has remained relevant after so many decades and has fostered unceasing brand loyalty because we continue to tap into women's emotions and desires, we continue to maintain a personal connection with them, and we continue to innovate through new technologies, colors, textures, and finishes.

Iconic brands and what they represent, no matter how many times they reinvent themselves, never go out of style. An integral part of OPI's vision has always been to help women express who they are, and who they want to be. Women will always want to express themselves through their fashion and beauty choices—that will never change. OPI responds by giving its consumers every color of the rainbow to represent the full spectrum of their personalities and beauty aspirations, along with a full range of textures and finishes based on the latest cutting-edge technologies. With our constant innovation, OPI still has the ability to generate excitement over and over again, despite being a mature brand.

> *OPI's vision has always been to help women reveal WHO THEY ARE and WHO THEY WANT TO BE.*

Iconic brands continually engage the culture's artifacts, infusing them with new meaning and keeping the brand on trend in new and unique ways. Take, for example, OPI's unique cross-branding partnerships. Even with the very best nail lacquer on the market, OPI would never have become an icon if it didn't transcend the bounds of a beauty product and connect with the wider culture. We never wanted to be *just* a beauty brand. We wanted to be a lifestyle brand; we wanted to be everywhere our customers were. So, with our cross-branding efforts we went out of our way to connect to many different aspects of popular culture. Now, watching your favorite movie, listening to your favorite recording artist, cheering on your favorite sports star, looking at the colors you've painted your room, drinking your favorite soft drink, or donating to your favorite charity can be an OPI experience. There is no other beauty brand in the world that touches the totality of cultural artifacts and the emotional desires of its consumer base like OPI does. This is one of the most important reasons we became iconic.

But perhaps the most important reason OPI became an icon is that our products, with their crazy names and gorgeous colors, tapped into the emotional heart of its fan base. My continuing task is to make OPI Nail Lacquer even more exciting and relevant to the consumer each and every season. My secret is that I am a woman, and I know how to get a woman's attention. For one thing, women love to tell stories, and I had a story they could relate to. I was a real person who had been through real struggles, a mom who was trying to juggle work and home and family, just like they were. I had similar anxieties, and similar guilt about not being Supermom. I also had the same desires our customers had when it came to beauty—I wanted a quick, easy, fun, and affordable way to make myself look and feel better. For me and for millions of other women, that was nails.

If there was anything that made me different from our customers, it was the thing that made me perfect for my job: my innate sense for color and color trends. I put that to work to create and curate all of those amazing colors that women loved and loved to wear. I spent hours and days and weeks and months on every single collection; I would not stop until each color was perfect for our consumers. I think that kind of dedication comes through in the products. I like to think that each bottle of OPI Nail Lacquer is infused with my deep intention to empower women, to give them the gift of beauty and luxury and confidence. To this day I look to the average woman as my color muse—she is the one I want to reach and to transform. The message I have to offer is as timeless as it is contemporary: a woman can be everything she wants to be with OPI.

And this is where story re-enters the picture: *the lacquers themselves* tell a story. There is the name of the lacquer, which is like the opening line to a story of adventure, food, travel, naughtiness, good fun, or laughter—or sometimes, all of the above! And then, of course, there is the color. The color a woman chooses instantly shares the full story of whatever she'd like to say to the world. She can be edgy. She can be glamorous. She can be flirtatious. She can be classic. She can be an iconoclast. She can make a difference. She can have fun with technology. She can be a part of pop culture. She can create, express, and dress to impress with OPI.

Today, the OPI brand has come to represent instant gratification, empowerment, self-expression, cutting-edge fashion, luxury, and fun for consumers all over the world—and these are people of vastly different backgrounds, cultures, and ages. If there's anything that tells me that OPI is an icon, it's that we've achieved inter-generational popularity. OPI is one of the very few fashion or beauty brands that erases the traditional bounds of age. Grandmothers, mothers, and daughters all wear OPI Nail Lacquer.

Today, my daughter and my mother are two of the primary women who inspire me. When Andrea was young I had the opportunity to see the world through her innocent eyes. As she's grown into a young woman, I've had the opportunity to see what has given her strength, what has helped her be assertive, and what has helped her be fearless in making her own decisions. My mother inspires me because she exemplifies what a woman can become: strong, generous, kind, and supportive.

These two women are like bookends on the journey of life. My daughter represents womanhood's ground zero. She is in the process of creating who she is in the world, in part through the consumer choices she makes. My mother represents the wise-woman stage of life, still loving beauty and its pleasures, though at a much deeper and soulful level. Both of these women want what OPI offers, just for different reasons. What is common to each is that looking good helps them feel empowered.

It's amazing to me that the brand has remained at the top of its category—it is still the number-one professional salon brand in the world—after so many decades. There are many product-related reasons we've achieved this, but not even OPI's now-legendary individual features and benefits—the logo, the bottle, the brush, the superior quality, and certainly the colors and the names—have made it an icon.

No, there's something deeper at work, and I think it comes back to the strong emotional bond between the OPI brand and its fans, and the bonds among the fans— the worldwide and vastly interconnected OPI Culture of Color. It is our fans who have enthusiastically woven OPI into all aspects of their lives, and they love sharing their experiences. Traditionally, the beauty industry tended to be product-centric, with a focus on the "hero" in the bottle, tube, or jar and the magical powers it was said to possess. OPI shifted the focus to the consumer and gave her all-new ways to interact with the brand and with her fellow OPI fans, the people partaking in the brand's aura and broadcasting it among their friends and on their social media platforms. The hunger for a personal connection between a consumer and her brand has never changed. What has changed is that now most of that connecting takes place online through social media. Now consumers the world over share their stories of who they are and who they are becoming with the help of these small yet powerful bottles of lacquer.

No Stopping Me Now

With our fans and their never-ending thirst for novelty, I don't think there's ever a time when I'm not seeking inspiration for new OPI colors and collections. Some part of my brain is always on, always scouting my surroundings

194 – I'M NOT REALLY A WAITRESS

for the next color inspiration. As I have since childhood, I pay attention to every instance of color and beauty in the natural world. I also take a look at what's happening on the runways of Milan and Paris and New York, I pore over fashion magazines, I think of delicious foods and flavors and beautiful fabrics, I look at what's happening in the world of interior design and architecture, I take note of the high-gloss finishes of luxury cars, I look at street fashion, I study fine art, I scan breaking trends on social media . . . and the list goes on. If it conveys beauty and color, it gets my attention.

> *The everyday woman has always been my muse. Inside every bottle of OPI Nail Lacquer is a message of female EMPOWERMENT, BEAUTY, and LUXURY.*

That said, although my color inspiration comes from so many of these external sources, my real inspiration comes from a place much deeper and more personal. My true muse is the everyday woman. I still design for her. It gives me great pleasure and the deepest inspiration to know that I am bringing color and luxury into the everyday woman's life.

I believe part of what quickly made OPI a branding phenomenon is that from the very beginning, we took the everyday woman seriously.

We saw how the nail care industry was missing the mark when it came to women's beauty needs and aspirations, and we responded by providing a line of products that exceeded their expectations and gave them a whole new vocabulary for beauty. When OPI gave nail lacquer a new image, we gave women a new opportunity to reinvent theirs. Inside each and every bottle of OPI Nail Lacquer is a message of female empowerment.

We saw that women always struggled with a shortage of time and were constantly called upon to juggle myriad roles—employee or employer, spouse or partner, caregiver to children or aging parents. We responded by giving her quick, effective beauty solutions to look and feel good. We gave her an affordable go-to luxury.

We saw that advertisers were failing to take women and their buying power seriously, so we changed the way beauty advertising was done, becoming the first professional beauty brand to advertise directly to the consumer. We avoided the common pitfall of trying to attract female customers by slapping on a "Make It Pink" attitude. Companies who really respect women and are working toward understanding the female consumer know that marketing to them requires a much more intelligent and nuanced approach. Increasingly, women won't settle for products that ignore or fail to fully meet their needs, or that do so only superficially. Women know when they are being stereotyped, underestimated, segmented by age or income, lumped together into an "all women" characterization, or worse, undifferentiated from men.

We saw that companies were failing to appreciate women's financial savvy, so we resolved to connect with women in a way that honored their financial intelligence as well as their role as CFO of their homes and families. Statistically, women influence most of the household spending decisions and are known to conduct more research before purchasing products than men. OPI gave women a sure bet of a product, whose results and whose beauty speak for themselves.

In our attitudes toward female consumers, OPI was again ahead of its time. Now in just a few short decades, we have all witnessed the birth of the female economy. According to the Gender Leadership Group, women influence 83 percent of all consumer spending in the United States and represent $7 trillion in annual spending. More than 57 percent of women participate in the US labor force, and the number of working women will soon surpass the number of working men. According to the 2017 State of Women-Owned Businesses Report, there are roughly 11.6 million women-owned businesses in the United States, and they generate more than $1.7 trillion in revenues. Women's yearly earning power rises annually, as does the number of women occupying senior positions. (As of April 2018, there were just twenty-four female CEOs on the Fortune 500 list. *Let's see more!*) Fortunately, marketing companies are putting more women in leadership positions—where they can help make key decisions and provide input about what does and doesn't resonate with women. Likewise, it makes sense that marketers are finally catching up with their customer base and giving female consumers the respect they deserve.

These women on the rise empower themselves with the choices they make for their families, their homes, and themselves—and that includes the beauty choices they make, from nail lacquer to hair products to fashion and functional accessories. OPI recognized this from the beginning, and our dedicated attention to the female consumer, the everyday woman who wants to look as good as she feels, is part of what made the brand iconic.

From Here to Eternity

By the mid-2000s, OPI was sold in more than one hundred countries and was a household name. It had become one of those iconic brands that was so widely recognized that its name was synonymous with the product. People now use "Tiffany lamp," for example, to refer to any stained leaded-glass lamp. The same goes for "Coca-Cola" or "Coke" for soft drinks, "Kleenex" for facial tissue, "Pampers" for diapers, or "Pond's" for cold cream.

We may have planted the seeds of an iconic brand, but it's OPI's LEGIONS OF LOYAL FANS who have brought it to maturity.

And of course, "OPI" for nail lacquer. Everybody knew that OPI stood for the best-quality, most revolutionary nail lacquer on the market, even if they had no idea that the letters O-P-I once stood for Ondontorium Products, Incorporated, the unwieldy moniker we'd dropped long ago.

As so many consumers gathered online and began to share their opinions and experiences, OPI's true aura emerged. The worldwide OPI Culture of Color loves sharing stories of how OPI Nail Lacquer has helped them mark and remember some of life's most meaningful occasions. They expanded the original OPI story by creating designs and styles and uses that far exceeded the products' original intended functions. They amplified the aura by broadcasting it far and wide and by creating meaningful connections between fellow nail color fans across the world. The OPI Culture of Color has become a living, breathing entity with myriad traditions and stories of its own. So we who created OPI planted the seeds of an iconic brand, but it was our fans who brought it to maturity.

Today, OPI is woven into the fabric of social consciousness. It has become a psychological, fashion-centric, and artistic phenomenon that is sustained among the millions of individual consumers who have come together in an extremely powerful collective. OPI is now a permanent part of the culture. Indeed, it is a cultural touchstone in itself.

OPI will continue to evolve into the future. Our entrepreneurial spirit and unconventional marketing strategies put OPI on the map. Our shared vision of empowerment and unlimited self-expression will drive us into the future, always coloring outside the lines of people's expectations. This spirit is what makes OPI extraordinary, revolutionary, and iconic, and it's what gives the OPI aura its transformative power.

The aura of the OPI brand transformed the concept of nail polish, and it went on to transform the nail care industry. It transformed nails into an exciting, always-hot fashion accessory. Most importantly, it gave women the ability to transform themselves.

And that, in a nutshell, is what makes OPI iconic.

— twelve —

ROSY FUTURE

I N 2010 GEORGE SCHAEFFER AND I FOUND OURSELVES sitting in a conference room full of executives at the headquarters of global beauty conglomerate Coty, Inc. The parent company of iconic fashion and beauty brands such as Marc Jacobs, Calvin Klein, Chloe, and, more recently, Alexander McQueen, Burberry, CoverGirl, Gucci, and Wella, Coty was our top choice for the company that would acquire OPI. They were a well-established, much-respected beauty company with a global presence, well-equipped to take OPI to the next level.

The decision to sell OPI was the result of a long and painful process, and though there were many factors that led to it, at the forefront was Miriam's divorce from George. Legal proceedings went on for years, and naturally, relations were sometimes strained. I felt heartbroken for my sister. Divorce is never easy on anyone, and in this case it was especially hard as we were such a close family, not to mention all deeply involved in a family business. Suffice it to say that things at the office were never quite the same after that, and finally George and I decided it was time to let the company go.

Coty showed us a great deal of respect throughout the sale and transition process. They really got OPI's vision, and they loved the brand. I chose to remain with OPI as a brand ambassador, designer, and consultant. I still create all the colors and collections, name the lacquers, and travel the world promoting the brand, and Coty gave me full creative latitude. They also agreed to let us keep operating at the North Hollywood OPI campus for another five years. Our employees could remain if they chose to, and if not they'd have plenty of time to make other plans. Most of them stayed.

Despite all these positive changes, and despite my continuing involvement at OPI, selling the company was heart-wrenching for me. The Monday after we'd signed off on everything I arrived early to a meeting at the Peninsula Hotel in Beverly Hills. I sat down in the bar area to wait, and my phone rang. It was the bank, calling to tell me that the transaction was complete—OPI was now owned by Coty. I thanked them and hung up quickly, overcome with emotion. Even though I knew the sale was a good thing and we were in good hands, I cannot describe how bereft I felt at that moment. I hardly knew what to do.

As it happened I had just been working with Serena Williams on her Grand Slam collection, and we had quickly developed a warm friendship. So on instinct I called her, and she picked up right away. I told her about the sale and how sad I was; I confessed that I wondered if we'd made a terrible mistake.

"Do you think it's too late," I sobbed, "to change our minds?"

Poor Serena. I'm sure this out-of-the-blue call from me was the last thing she was expecting. But true to form, she rose to the occasion.

"Oh, Suzi, don't be sad!" she said. "There's going to be a new chapter in your life and it will be even better. You wait and see."

Of course I wasn't *entirely* in earnest about changing our minds, but my grief was genuine and deep. OPI had been my life's passion for nearly three decades. When I was young I thought I would work in a research lab. Instead I took the curiosity and rigor of a researcher and applied it to creating colors in the OPI R&D lab. I had poured so much time and creative energy into OPI, had watched it grow from a tiny dental supply company housed in a shoebox of a building to the number-one professional salon brand in the world. It was one of those success stories you couldn't make up if you tried. And personally, I had gone from sweeping the floors and hand-filling bottles to being the First Lady of Nails, co-founder and leader of a multimillion-dollar business.

Moreover, I had really come to love our employees, many of whom had made OPI their lifelong careers. At our very first exploratory meeting with Coty, the *least* senior manager present was a seventeen-year veteran. Some of our employees had been with us for more than twenty years, such as Ilene "Little Stuff" Richkind, and a few, such as Bryan Stein, for more than thirty. There was no task Ilene couldn't do, from organizing trade shows and events (and even my children's bat and bar mitzvahs) to eventually managing our entire customer service department. Bryan, too, was an absolute treasure, as knowledgeable about anything IT-related as he was about business. Our employees were the backbone of the company, and I looked on them all as family. In a final gesture of gratitude, George and I forgave the $300,000 in loans that remained outstanding from employees who'd borrowed money from us.

Though the sale of OPI brought in more money than any of us had ever dreamed of, some things remained exactly the same. My husband George and I still drove the kids to school, went to their sports events, bought the groceries, cooked dinner, attended synagogue, had Shabbat dinner with the ex-

Every good leader should HAVE A DETAILED SUCCESSION PLAN— even if you don't have any plans to leave soon. You never know what could happen, and it's a sign of leadership to plan for the unexpected and have a succession plan in place.

tended family. We still insisted that our kids keep a budget and that they dedicate money to charity. And my greatest fear about no longer being in the driver's seat—*what on earth would I do with myself?*—proved baseless. Though I was no longer co-owner of OPI, I was as busy as ever as OPI's principal creator and brand ambassador, which is how I wanted it.

Not only do I simply love to work—I'm quite at a loss when my plate isn't full—staying so busy distracted me from the grief of handing over the reins. Even though it was time to move on and I had full confidence in my successor, Jill Bartoshevich, who's now been with OPI for nearly twenty years, a sense of loss was inevitable. What a strange, discombobulating day that was, when I no longer sat at the head of the table, no longer ran the meetings, no longer made the final decisions! But by then I was so comfortable with myself and what I'd achieved, not to mention so confident in Jill's leadership, that I was very much content to step back and let someone else be up front. My new role was going to be very different, but no less fun and exciting.

Meanwhile, George Schaeffer was already exploring other business options, and after a couple of years, he moved on. He is a true entrepreneur with a restless spirit, and he left to pursue his other interests, including his haircare brand, the insurance industry, and his philanthropic work.

Then after five years, it was time for the North Hollywood campus to shut down. In December 2015 the main OPI factory relocated to Sanford, North Carolina, where operating costs were much lower. (The R&D team and the executive offices are now at a new location in Los Angeles.) Many of our long-term employees chose to retire at that point. Alicia, who worked in shipping, was one. When I asked her about her future plans, her face broke into a wide smile. "Miss Suzi," she said, "I'm going to go to the gym every day, learn better English, and enjoy my life." Brava, Alicia. May you enjoy every day. Over and over as employees left the campus for the last time, they grasped my hands or reached out to hug me. Over and over, I heard this: "Thank you. Thank you. God bless you. You changed my family's life. Thank you." I barely made it through the day.

The next day the movers arrived to start hauling off all the factory equipment. It took one hundred tractor trailers to transport it all. It was time for that new chapter Serena assured me would come.

And it turned out she was right.

Withstands the Test of Thyme

In addition to creating the OPI lacquers and collections and helping to name them, I'm also still actively involved with working with incredible talent from film, television, music, and sports who partner with OPI as its brand ambassadors. In 2016, for example, I teamed up with Kerry Washington for the Washington, D.C., collection. Kerry is an absolutely beautiful person inside and out and incredibly smart. In all these years, she was the one celebrity I was nervous to meet, and to make matters worse, her manager Katherine was rumored to be very intimidating. But I had long admired Kerry and really wanted to work with her. So we arranged to meet at her agency, and I sat down with Kerry and her agent and her purportedly scary manager. Despite my anxiety I proceeded as I would with any other meeting: I just told my story and the story of OPI, much the same way I'd done at Coca-Cola.

Thankfully it had the same effect. They were on board immediately and said let's make this happen. Kerry was an absolute dream to work with and even sent me flowers after her OPI photo shoot. (Isn't it supposed to be the other way around?!) And I'm happy to say that she *and* her manager, who turned out to be quite lovely, are now good friends of mine.

So, yes, I may no longer sweep the floors, but I still go to work. And without the executive leadership responsibilities and the grueling back-to-back international trips, I have more time to myself than I've had in decades. It's certainly not all bad! I am relishing the time I'm able to spend with my mother, and as her health declines I am more involved in her daily care. I am also able to spend more time with my beloved sister and my fantastic husband and kids, and I'm enjoying every moment, especially the big milestones like planning for my daughter's wedding. I've had the chance to relax, to read, to do more community and charitable work, and to focus on writing the story of OPI, a goal I've had for more than a decade now. I've even had a few facials, something I didn't have time for in more than twenty years!

My newest passion is passing on all the things I've learned to the next generation of entrepreneurs and business leaders. I'm frequently invited to speak at various functions and events, and I have found that I absolutely *love* to inspire and educate young people. This is quite an evolution for someone who used to dread the spotlight in any form or fashion and who was terrified of public speaking.

> *One of the best ways to give back is to PASS ON YOUR WISDOM to the next generations.*

In Hebrew there is a term called *shoah*. It means to remember. Each succeeding generation has the duty to remember the traditions and to pass them on to the next generation. At home, that means my husband and I raised our children with the principles and traditions of Judaism, and we told them the stories of our families so they will remember and preserve them and eventually pass them on to their own children. Likewise in the professional arena, elder generations have a responsibility to pass down their institutional knowledge and everything they know about how to succeed. It has often been said that our children are our greatest investment, and it is true. But the same principle applies in business: Training and inspiring the next generations of leaders is a responsibility to take seriously. It ensures their personal success as well as the company's.

Now I routinely find myself standing before large audiences. I feel so passionate about passing on what I've learned over the course of a long and fulfilling career that my enthusiasm overcomes any remaining nerves. Gratitude is just as motivating. I have been given so much and have grown so much as a person through this thirty-seven-year journey with OPI—how could I not give back?

So here is a distillation of my best advice for people just getting started. I offer this to business audiences, but as you'll see, many of these principles have universal application.

I believe WE GET ONE SHOT AT LIFE, and we should GO AT IT WITH ALL WE'VE GOT. At the end of the journey, do you want to look back and admire how you always colored within the lines? No—you want to look back and feel great about taking some risks that brought you a life of passion and fulfillment.

1. **Trust your instincts and recognize opportunity**. Be prepared to see possibilities in unexpected places. Who knew that a dental supply company would lead to the iconic brand OPI is today? Not everyone will agree with you all of the time, so you must be able to trust yourself and go where the opportunity leads you.

2. **Start now**. Another way of saying this is YOLO! You Only Live Once. Each one of us has been touched by a loved one facing his or her last days on earth. There really isn't any time for putting off your dreams and what you want to make of this life.

3. **Start from the heart**. Tap into your heart and find a passion. Find something that you care about deeply, and fight tirelessly to achieve your goals. Conversely,

don't waste time on something you're not passionate about. If your heart isn't in the journey, you won't be able to muster the strength to continue, especially when you encounter adversity along the way.

4. **Avoid borrowing money**. If it's at all possible, don't rely on loans to start your business. George and I were typical Europeans, leery of borrowing. The caution is justified. Not borrowing means you won't have the stress of repaying loans and paying interest on top of that. And it's not wise to get yourself overextended before you even make your first sale. When you do make money, invest earnings right back into the business.

5. **Never give up**. Calvin Coolidge said it well: "Perseverance is everything." Life and business can be difficult, as we all know. But if you give up prematurely, you'll never know what doors would have opened down the road. Remember that your successes come from your struggles. Some people will stop when they meet the first roadblock. But successful people keep plugging away.

6. **Conquer fear**. If you are frightened to do something, it usually means you should do it. Growth always comes from facing the thing that frightens you, feeling the fear—and then doing it anyway. Don't forget that the more you avoid fearful situations, the stronger the fear becomes. But the more you embrace what frightens you, the stronger your courage becomes.

7. **Have a story**. People connect with you and are persuaded by you when you have an engaging story to tell. Whether you're telling a personal story or the story of your product, service, or company, speak with conviction and passion—and also with concision and relatability. Some of the best parts of life are when we get together and tell our stories and gain wisdom and inspiration from each other.

8. **Don't waste people's time**. When Harris and I pitched super-busy fashion and beauty editors, we had a game plan: we gave them a good story, we chose good restaurants, and we gave them free samples of the product. Boom, boom, boom. Quick and effective and memorable. We never disappointed, and everyone always showed up.

9. **Lead by example**. You can never expect from others what you can't expect from yourself. Never lose sight of your role as the example *par excellence* and your employees' inspiration.

10. **Cultivate being well-rounded**. The successful businessperson is not a narrow specialist. She knows and understands all aspects of the business. She can spot a bottleneck as quickly as an accounting error; she can rectify a weakness in a sales campaign as easily as a flaw in personnel management. But when things go wrong, as they will from time to time . . .

11. **Assume ultimate responsibility**. If you are in a management position, solicit opinions and advice from your direct reports and customers, and listen with an

open mind. But remember that the final decision lies with you, as does the responsibility for all outcomes. If something goes amiss, promptly own the mistake and get to work to fix it.

12. **Manage your time**. How you handle your time is one of the most important aspects of being successful. If you don't plan your day and prioritize tasks, your calendar and your tasks will control you, rather than the other way around.

13. **Set aside time for thinking**. We live in a culture that values busyness. But why do we need to appear busy every single second of the day? Some things require stillness and thought, such as birthing new ideas and problem solving. Let your mind wander; you'll be surprised by the ideas that naturally bubble to the surface if you give them some breathing room.

14. **Accept the zigs and the zags**. When you start a journey, expect to find mountains to climb, valleys to traverse, and zigs and zags that take you off the expected course. What's important is that you keep going, and that you develop resilience and flexibility so that you can get up in the morning and start again.

15. **Revel in the limelight—graciously**. Enjoy it when things go well and the light shines on you. But the person whose career moves from success to success is the one who also knows the meaning of humility. So don't get dazzled by the light when you're at the top. Believe me, there is always an opportunity just around the corner to fall flat on your face.

16. **LOL.** Laugh out loud! Enjoy yourself. If you're miserable at work and it's not due to some sort of personality conflict, it's probably a sign that you're not passionate about what you're doing. Polish up that résumé and hit the job market. Life is too short not to LOL every day.

17. **Be grateful and say thank you.** It is a privilege to have the opportunity to pursue your dreams and try to make a difference in this world. Each and every one of us has the capacity to make the world a better place than we found it, and this is an occasion for gratitude. So is a job well done—never forget to thank your employees for their efforts.

18. **Give back.** Some people fall into the trap of thinking that if they can't make a huge difference they just won't try. But helping even one person is enough. You never know when your efforts with one person will go on to affect the greater good of the world. Every day, I wake up and think of *tzedakah* and wonder how I can make a difference.

19. **Respect people.** This one may seem obvious, but in light of what's happening in public discourse today it's a needed reminder. In all aspects of your life, business or personal, in person or online, treat people with respect. I treated my employees, my business associates, and my children with respect, and in turn they respected me.

20. **Most important: cherish your family**. The demands of business can be tremendous, but remember why

you're doing all of this. Give your family your time and your love and your guidance. They are your anchor in this crazy, wonderful world, and you are theirs.

My general philosophy on life and business is aptly summarized in this quote from artist Alex Noble: "Success is not a place at which one arrives, but rather the spirit with which one undertakes and continues the journey." I believe we get one shot at this life, and we should throw ourselves into it with all we've got! When all is said and done, do you want to look back and admire how you habitually played it safe and always colored within the lines? No—you want to look back and feel great about taking some risks that paid off, risks that brought you a life of passion and fulfillment. I love the way writer Hunter S. Thompson put it—though I've put my own spin on his famous quote: "Life shouldn't be a journey to the grave with the intention of arriving safely in an attractive and well-preserved body, but rather to skid in sideways, chocolate in one perfectly manicured hand, champagne in the other, body thoroughly used up, totally worn out and screaming, 'Wooo-hooooo . . . what a ride!'"

Berry On Forever

The aura of OPI is now far vaster than I ever could have imagined or hoped for. It exists beyond me, beyond George, beyond even the brand itself, because of the millions and millions of OPI fans all over the world who have taken up the mantle and created something new and invigorating for themselves. Their creativity is amazing to behold. If you want to see true artists at work, go to your favorite social media sites and search nail art hashtags and see what people are doing with OPI products. (I've been particularly surprised and delighted by how nail artists are using negative space and leaving part of the nail naked, a trend you now see reflected in fashion as well. I love it.) Or check out what's happening with classic looks—an elegant French manicure, a bold red that pops, the beautiful blush of a neutral—and you'll find plenty of beauty and inspiration. The variety of what you can achieve with OPI is much of the point: we gave women the tools and the means to choose from any hue of the rainbow and to express themselves in any way they wished.

We also expanded the conversation far beyond "nail polish" or a single, self-contained beauty product. Instead, what's possible with OPI Nail Lacquer goes well beyond the constraints of a half-ounce bottle. It represents travel, food, escape, dreams, self-expression, luxury, aspirations. It gives people a small but powerful tool to show the world who they are and who they want to be.

> *Women who have found their voice and their personal style and sense of self are women who BREAK BARRIERS and CHANGE THE WORLD.*

Women who have found their voice and their personal style and sense of self are women who break barriers and change the world.

That certainly happened for me. Through OPI, I was able to find my true voice and my purpose in life and make a lasting difference. Because of OPI, my life has been an adventure I never, in my wildest dreams, could have imagined. I mean it from the bottom of my heart when I say *If I can do this, anybody can*. It is entirely within your grasp to create your own life of passion, fulfillment, creativity, and success. If I can do it, anyone can!

So now, for thirty-seven years (and counting), I've worked to satisfy our consumers' thirst for color in every imaginable hue, dimension, and texture. I am so grateful that I continue to have a very unique opportunity to help people achieve their aspirations by feeling more confident in themselves through OPI—and I am excited about what the next decades will bring. "Take the first step in faith," Martin Luther King Jr. said. "You don't have to see the whole staircase, just take the first step." These are words I have long cherished. In a nutshell, that's how we created and built the best nail care company in the business. We took one step and then another, and another, and another, feeling our way through each and every one. Accomplishment is a long journey that is built on small, daily acts of faith that build into a beautiful outcome of a larger vision. OPI taught me to dare to take the staircase even though I couldn't see the steps. It inspired me to be bold enough to reinvent the beauty category. The result is unrivaled love and loyalty for our brand.

So when I speak to audiences, it doesn't matter if it's an auditorium of six hundred MBA students or a thousand executives from the beauty and fashion industries or a dozen seniors at a local high school. I go in with confidence and gratitude, and I tell my story of overcoming tremendous odds to become the person standing before them today.

I tell the story of how George Schaeffer and I, along with the most dedicated and loyal employees in the world, saw our dreams come true.

I tell an immigrant story, of fleeing a place of oppression and fear and starting over from scratch—not once but twice. Of working very, very hard to learn a language and a culture and make a living.

I tell them a story of family. Of how I was shaped by loving, generous parents. Of how I was able to become a leader in a male-dominated industry *and* be a fully engaged wife and mother through the unwavering support of my parents Laszlo and Magda Weiss, my sister Miriam, and my husband, Dr. George Fischmann. I tell a story of my children, Andrea and Andrew, who are my joy and my constant inspiration.

I tell them a story of women's empowerment. Of how I evolved from a timid, awkward, shy schoolgirl who barely spoke to the business leader known worldwide as Suzi the First Lady of Nails. And of how women everywhere are able to use OPI's products to express their individual styles and personalities and to feel more confident and beautiful.

I tell them the story of an industry disruptor. Of how OPI changed the conversation of nails and elevated the entire industry. Of how it brought beauty and color and luxury to everyone, of how it made color and self-expression exciting and sexy, of how it made salon manicures relevant and essential.

I tell them all the story of success born of passion and tenacity and hard work. And of overwhelming, joyful love.

ACKNOWLEDGMENTS

LIKE RUNNING A BUSINESS, WRITING A BOOK ISN'T POSSIble without a dedicated team, and I'd like to thank mine. Each person played an instrumental role in bringing *I'm Not Really a Waitress* to life on the page.

To my husband Dr. George Fischmann, whose support has been unceasing and his patience unparalleled. Thank you for supporting me in whatever I do and for being the most loving, amazing, super-smart father. You are the best role model anyone could hope for and forever my love.

To my daughter Andrea, who has grown from a gangly tomboy who despised nail polish to an amazing young woman who always calls to tell me about her latest nail color (and everything else). Thank you for being my joy and my greatest inspiration. You make me want to be better each and every day.

To my son Andrew, a voracious reader and the nicest young man I know. Thank you for your passion for reading, which has always inspired me, and for your encouragement as I tried my hand at writing. Both were invaluable in making this book happen. Your kindness, thoughtfulness, and loyalty are truly exceptional.

To my son-in-law Jacob, talented chef and real estate agent and the newest addition to our family. Thank you for being there for all of us and for taking care of all the details. I admire you for succeeding in whatever you do—especially your greatest success in choosing to marry my daughter.

To my sister Miriam Schaeffer, whom I can call for any sort of help at any hour. Thank you for always saying yes. Thank you for keeping the family together and upholding our traditions.

To George Schaeffer, my greatest mentor. Thank you for your guidance, your vision, and your boundless energy. Together we changed the beauty industry.

To my niece and nephew, Nicole Schaeffer and Robbie Schaeffer. Thank you for your lasting love and respect. I love you both like my own.

To Harris Shepard, PR genius, who endured my abuse for so many years and somehow remains my best friend. We grew up together and we made history. What a team we were! Thank you for being the best public relations professional in the business.

To my book partner Catherine Knepper, an amazing writer. Thank you for telling my story in the most beautiful words. You helped make my long-held dream of writing my story come true.

To my literary agent Jill Marsal, the best in the business. Thank you for believing in me and in my story. Without you none of this would have happened.

To my editor Laura Mazer, gifted guide. From our first conversation I knew I was in good hands. Thank you for helping me polish these pages.

To all the women and men who worked at OPI, my dear OPI family. There are no better employees anywhere. Thank you for making all of this possible, and for creating one of the best beauty brands in the world.

To my new family at Coty, Inc., who immediately caught the OPI vision and ran with it. Special thanks to President of Professional Beauty Sylvie Moreau-Lepeigneul and Chief Marketing Officer of Professional Beauty Laura Simpson for allowing me to use the OPI Lacquer names in this book.

Thank you to my dear parents, Laszlo and Magda Weiss. To my dad, who passed away fifteen years ago, you are the example *par excellence* of a brave, loving, hard-working father who would do anything for family. I think of you every day and am so grateful for you. And to my mommy, Magda Weiss, my hero, my all. We usually think of heroes as towering figures, but though you are the tiniest person, you walk in grandeur. Thank you for teaching me humility, love, kindness, and gratitude. Thank you for your most amazing meals and your tireless dedication to family.

Finally, thank you to all the women around the world who love OPI and have made it a household name. Thank you for being my muse, my inspiration, my motivation, my source of joy. Thank you for allowing me into your lives through one bottle of nail lacquer after another. Together, we told an amazing story.

ABOUT THE AUTHOR

KNOWN WORLDWIDE AS THE "FIRST LADY OF NAILS," OPI co-founder and brand ambassador Suzi Weiss-Fischmann initially made her mark on the beauty industry in 1989, when she created the first thirty OPI nail lacquers. Thanks to her keen eye for color, several of these shades still remain bestsellers in OPI's classics collection, including OPI Red, Malaga Wine, and Coney Island Cotton Candy.

In her thirty-seven years at OPI, Suzi has continued to set trends for the nail industry. She ignited the dark nail revolution with the deep purple Lincoln Park After Dark, was the first to add real diamond dust to nail lacquer, and mainstreamed nail art with Shatter by OPI.

Suzi has created thousands of iconic OPI shades, including You Don't Know Jacques!, Russian Navy, Bubble Bath, and Cajun Shrimp. I'm Not Really a Waitress, one of her best-known colors, has been heralded as the perfect shade of red by women across the globe. *Allure* inducted this lacquer into its Beauty Hall of Fame in 2011, after it won the Best Nail Polish award nine times.

Suzi's work not only makes its way into each bottle of OPI Nail Lacquer, her name is featured on many of her creations. Every seasonal collection includes a namesake shade as a nod to its renowned designer. Some of the most recent hues include Suzi—The First Lady of Nails (Washington, DC Collection), Suzi Nails New Orleans (New Orleans Collection), O Suzi Mio (Venice Collection), Suzi and the Arctic Fox (Iceland Collection), and Suzi Chases Portu-geese (Lisbon Collection).

Suzi pioneered the development of OPI partnerships, elevating consumers' overall brand experience. Under her guidance, OPI became the first nail care brand to collaborate with Hollywood's top films and celebrities, as well as iconic companies including Coca-Cola, Dell, and Ford.

As brand ambassador, Suzi serves as the voice of OPI, the world's largest professional nail brand. Suzi is the go-to authority for beauty editors and fashion designers alike, regularly contributing to stories both in the United States and internationally about nail care and color trends. She has been featured in numerous magazines such as

W, More, Family Circle, and *Martha Stewart Living* and has appeared on top television programs including *The Today Show* (NBC) and *Nightline* (ABC). A native of Hungary, Suzi now makes her home in Los Angeles with her husband and two children.